A LIFE IN GOLF

Inspirations & Insights from Australia's Greatest Golfer

The Slattery Media Group Pty Ltd
Level 39/385 Bourke Street, Melbourne
Victoria, Australia, 3000

Published by The Slattery Media Group, 2005, 2013

This updated and revised edition published by The Slattery Media Group Pty Ltd, 2018

Cover image: Peter Thomson with his daughter Peta-Ann (Pan), after winning the 1967 Australian PGA Championship at Melbourne's Metropolitan GC. (©Thomson family collection).

A catalogue record for this book is available from the National Library of Australia

Group Publisher: Geoff Slattery
Art Director, Cover Design and Typeset: Kate Slattery
Illustrations: Bill Wood

Printed in Australia by Griffin Press

slatterymedia.com

A LIFE IN GOLF

Inspirations & Insights from Australia's Greatest Golfer

PETER THOMSON AO, CBE

with **STEVE PERKIN**

Foreword by Geoff Ogilvy, 2006 US Open Champion.

An updated and revised edition of
Lessons I Have Learned:
Inspirations & Insights
from Australia's Greatest Golfer
(2005)

visit *slatterymedia.com*

‘There are no superfluous sentences between the covers of this book. Instead, with Peter’s usual economy of words and outstanding knowledge of golf, there are insights and lessons for the benefit of all golfers.’

Richie Benaud, former Australian cricket captain, journalist and broadcaster

Tributes to Peter Thomson, AO, CBE (1929–2018)

‘*I always respected Peter Thomson the golfer.
Later in life, I respected & appreciated Peter Thomson
the man even more. Five-time Open champ, three-time
Presidents Cup captain and always a proud Australian.
We have lost a special member of golf's global family.*’

Jack Nicklaus

‘*Peter Thomson was a truly wonderful golfer
& a fine global ambassador for our game.
His contribution to golf will not be forgotten.
In addition he was the most intellectual &
best read player I ever met.*’

Gary Player

‘*There have been many individuals who have
touched the game of golf, none more so than Peter Thomson
in his era. His life off the course deserves equal distinction,
having transitioned to a scribe for The Age, then politics,
which is not something many golfers before or after
him have accomplished.*’

Greg Norman

‘*Australia has lost a golfing legend and my hero.
Australian golf thanks you for your iconic presence
& valuable guidance over the years.*’

Ian Baker-Finch.

A Vision of the Future

‘Peter Thomson, the 19-year-old Brunswick youth, who, on Saturday, won the Victorian amateur golf championship at Woodlands, is a “smiling, happy, human kid”.

Young Peter has tremendous possibilities as a golfer. I believe he could become the best Australian to play the game. He seems to have everything needed, and to have everything in a big way.

Perhaps the most pleasing possession, in addition to his grand temperament, is a most disarming and intriguing modesty.

To a greater degree, probably, than any former champion, Peter “plays golf”. It’s his fun, not his work.

With one of the most fluent, easy and artistic swings, he is efficiently personalised when he has a golf club in his hands.

When Peter puts his hands on a club, they caress it and, similarly, when he stands to address a ball his feet “feel” the turf.’

J.M. (Jack) Dillon, writing in *The Herald*, Melbourne, in 1948

Photo by Bryn Campbell/The Observer/Getty Images

Peter Thomson at the Piccadilly World Match Play Championships, Wentworth, Surrey (October 14, 1967).

FOREWORD

See the target, hit the target

By Geoff Ogilvy

I grew up in Melbourne. A wonderful place to grow up for a slightly golf-obsessed kid. I was a member of Victoria Golf Club, one of the famed Melbourne Sandebelt courses. I spent most of my formative years playing Victoria and, when I could, the other great courses in the area, such as Royal Melbourne and Kingston Heath. My Australian golf heroes in those days were players like Greg Norman and Steve Elkington, but as time went on I started to realise that perhaps the one to admire most was Peter Thomson.

The clubhouse at Victoria is a wonderful old building that has been there since the course was built. It is a great clubhouse, which has come through a few renovations retaining most of its character. It is almost museum-like in spots, and has wonderful photos and memorabilia from all the important golfers to have been members there.

I noticed very quickly that Peter was seen as the club's most famous and best playing member. The club's pride in 'Thommo' and his achievements is obvious as soon as you walk in the front door.

Peter won more than 90 titles all around the world, including five Open Championships. A truly international player, he played everywhere, but he especially loved to play in Britain— the game played on its finest seaside courses perfectly suited his style and temperament. He is one of the best ever to play those wonderful old courses. Courses and conditions that are always a good measure of a player's game. Living in St Andrews for a lot of his life, he is truly respected and loved in Scotland, as not only a five-time winner of their biggest championship, but as a true champion for the traditions of the game.

He was one of the pioneers in Asia as well, playing in places like India and Indonesia. He was one of the first to support their new fledgling events, playing a role in the game's development in the region. He didn't play in America as much as some may have liked, a criticism for some but not for me. The soft lush courses presented there required a game played almost completely in the air. A game that Peter understood, and could play well enough, but a game that I don't think he enjoyed at all. He chose to play the game he enjoyed playing, which is hardly a thing to criticise.

Anyway, his record when playing the new seniors tour in America in the mid-1980s proved his ability to adapt to any conditions, and compete well anywhere he played. He won nine times one year with the new 50 and overs, showing he was still the man to beat wherever he played.

This book of stories and excerpts from interviews with Thomson is a wonderful read. Perhaps one of golf's best ever thinkers, his words have a way of making a game we all make too complicated seem so much simpler. You see, the game for Thomson is a simple matter: see a target and, while avoiding hazards, hit to the target.

Why worry about anything else? So this is not an instruction book, though there is much to learn for everyone here, it is just a glimpse into a mind that sees the game differently to most of us. Better than most of us.

I certainly wish I had got some of this advice when a younger golfer. I would definitely be better off today if I had. Most would, I think.

Thomson has been involved in the game of golf for more than 60 years; playing, watching, teaching and designing courses around the globe. He is a true student of the game, with a lifetime of lessons to share.

Australia's greatest golfer gets to have his say here, and we should all listen.

—Geoff Ogilvy, 2006 US Open Champion

Getty Images

At Walton Heath in 1960.

INTRODUCTION

By Steve Perkin

I am writing this on June 20, 2018, the day of Peter Thomson's death. He was 88.

The news broke this morning. It was no surprise, as Peter hadn't been well, but it was impossible not to feel a deep sadness. It was 13 years ago that I started working on this book project with Peter. I first broached the idea with him in 2005. He wanted to write it himself, but as I got to know him better, it became clear he would never find the time to sit down at his beloved laptop and craft the words. He did, however, have time to talk. Why he allowed me such access, I'll never now know.

Every few days back in 2005, I would meet him at the Melbourne office of Thomson, Wolveridge, Perrett, for 30 or 40 minutes and throw topics at him. He would talk and I'd go away and transcribe the tapes, word for word. There was no need to edit them because Peter Thomson was as clinical and precise with his words as he was with a long iron into a green.

We adopted the same approach for this revision, in 2013. I threw more up-to-date golfing issues at Peter and he gave his opinions.

During one of our meetings, he showed me his scrapbook, a massive tome lovingly started by his first wife, Lois, and continued by his second wife, Mary. Among the many photos were his Order of the British Empire certificate signed by Queen Elizabeth II, a telegram from his political hero, Sir Robert Menzies, and another from Ian Fleming, the creator of James Bond. Items, which people like you and I would frame and hang on a study wall, were gathered, unassumingly, in a scrapbook that I doubt he opened more than once or twice.

I can only hope that this scrapbook is saved and adopted by the State Library or Golf Australia for it is a remarkable record of a remarkable story.

Peter never wrote an instructional book. During his own career, he never saw the need to read the views of others on how the game should be played, not because he thought himself better, but because it confused his mind. The game was, for the man dubbed "Peerless Pete" or "Perfect Pete" or "Five Times", quite a simple matter—see a target and, avoiding potential trouble, hit to the target. How does one fill a book when the subject in question is so straightforward?

And if you ever had the honour of playing with him, he never offered advice. My theory on this is that he only ever saw the game in its simplest form, so he probably figured you'd be able to work it out for yourself.

So this book is as close to an instructional book as Peter Thomson ever wrote. It also includes edited extracts from articles he wrote over many years as a golfing columnist, first with the now defunct Melbourne *Herald*, and since then *The Age*, as well as *Golf Digest* magazine and other assorted magazines and books. These extracts have been included first, because they stand the test of time, and, second, because of their clarity and simplicity.

But overriding all that, we have included them in this book because they deserve to be recorded, just as Peter deserves to be recognised with a book that honours his contribution, not only to Australian golf, but to the international game.

And he was an "international" golfer in the true sense. The winner of more than 90 titles, among them five British Opens, Thomson was sometimes criticised for not playing more golf in America than he did—criticised by Americans who may have felt cheated and Australians who wanted to see him take on the world's best. But nobody in Japan will criticise Thomson. Nor in Indonesia. Nor in India. Nor in Hong Kong. Nor in Thailand. Nor in New Zealand. Thomson supported the game in these areas by playing their fledgling events and taking his mates to play them as well.

Nor will you find a Scotsman prepared to criticise him, because like few other golfers of his generation or any other, Thomson respected the game's roots, upheld its traditions and loved its birthplace, St Andrews.

No, it matters not whether this man was the finest player this country has produced. It matters not whether he was the finest player of his generation or the finest player outside America. What matters only is that this man loved the game, loved it until his death, and always saw the game differently from the rest of us. And for all these reasons, he deserves to have his say.

Steve Perkin, June 2018

This book includes material drawn from transcripts of interviews between Peter Thomson and Steve Perkin, plus excerpts from articles written by Peter Thomson, or from interviews conducted by him, and published in newspapers and magazines over seven decades.

A FASCINATING GAME

Every time you play golf, you are playing against something, either another golfer or the par or your own handicap score. At first, it was a big hurdle for me to break the 100, then my target was 90, and so on until I could score in the 60s sometimes. In improving gradually like this, I came to realise the main obstacle you must overcome is yourself, and this is what makes golf such a fascinating game. A game you can never absolutely master and a game you will never tire of.

FROM CRADLE TO GRAVE

Golf is a unique game that can be played from the cradle to the grave. It involves the whacking of a small ball across varied terrain of "fair ground" and unfavourable areas called hazards. The stages of the arena on which it is played come to an end when the ball is gently struck into a jam tin-sized hole on a nice smooth patch called a "green". The rest of it is more social than sporting and, in the end, it doesn't matter what the score is. Winning and losing are abstract terms. As dreamy as it may seem, golf can be a frustrating activity, as it plays upon our human nature, bringing out the silly side. We all think we can play better than we can, and none of us has a madder conceit than a septuagenarian trying to pull off what he could do in his glory 40 years back.

The Age, Melbourne, November 25, 2004

THERE'S NO ONE 'WAY'

I have seen many a young player start on the wrong foot, taught by somebody who says there is a "way" to play golf. There is no "way". There are the same number of ways as there are people who play golf. If I think of all the champions I've played against ... Lee Trevino was different from Sam Snead, who was different from Ben Hogan, Julius Boros, Cary Middlecoff, Henry Cotton, and our own Norman von Nida and Kel Nagle ... there's not one swing, there's a variety. Only the essence is the same—get the ball to go where you want it to go.

FEELING THE WAY

Sam Snead once gave me a wonderful tip. He told me, on the downswing the longer you take to get to the ball, the farther you will hit it. It's just a feeling—you wouldn't vary one 10/1000ths of a second—but it's the feeling of not rushing that's the trick.

Golf Digest, 1994

A MIND GAME

Golf is at least a 50 per cent mental game and if you recognise that it is the mind that prompts us physically, then you can almost say that golf is entirely a mental effort. Certainly the difference between winning and losing is always a mental one. The mistakes that are made that lose a match are always made in the mind. The brilliant shots that win matches have their origin and inspiration at the mental level.

The total mental effort needed for winning golf events can be summed up in one word—concentration. Proper concentration wins matches. Poor concentration loses.

The Secrets of Australia's Golfing Success, published 1961

COMPETING

I was a very hungry competitor. Just because I had a smile on my face didn't mean I wasn't a pretty hungry golfer. I think I was as competitive as any. That came from instinct, I used to fight in the schoolyards to get my own way. It was born and bred in me.

National Club Golfer, 2014

MAKING IT BETTER

We are all imitators. We are each a huge database of observation and information accumulated and filed over our lifetime. It is from this collection and re-collection that we draw in our creative mood. What we have seen that stimulates us, looms large in our minds.

So it is with golf course planners. We have our own passions and idols as any other artists. We follow examples which strike us as worthy. And we each feel an urge to impose our will. Thus it is that courses are born, holes extended, upgraded, faults perceived corrected, and generally, following our craft.

If all goes well, with support, something is achieved. If support fails, we fail. All our dreams are lost.

We have then an experience that either makes or breaks us. Do we exist to entertain the golf world? Or do we trade to educate and persuade? I like to think the latter.

Golf Architecture Magazine, 1997

TRUST IN NATURE

Draw the club straight back. Never mind about what the books din into you about turns and pivots. Just draw it straight back as far as is comfortable and let nature take its course. Don't turn away. Just draw it back, but keep your weight squarely on both feet and don't sway.

Whatever type of flight your swing gives your shots, be content to do the same thing every time you swing and hit the same typeof shot. At least then you will know where the ball will end up after you've hit it.

The Secrets of Australia's Golfing Success, published 1961

SNEAD AND HOGAN

Hogan was very complicated. I don't know what he was on about, he would always hit hundreds of practice balls. Sam's (Snead) first shot in a day would be perfect, he didn't need any practice.

PLAY HOLES FOR PRACTICE

My first steps in golf were at Royal Park Golf Course in inner-city Melbourne, across the street from where I lived. Fortunately, the course was empty because it was the beginning of World War II; all the men were away and very few women played, so, as a boy of 13 or 14, I had a golf course to myself. I didn't have a full set of clubs, but individual clubs had been thrust at me from various sources and I used them as best I could, although I never had more than two golf balls.

If I had time after school, from 4.30 to dark, I played a few holes with the two balls and, in hindsight, it was the best possible training I could have had. Golf is about making a score, and with those two balls, I tried to make fours on the par fours and threes on the par threes. I didn't succeed for a while ... I'd make fives and sixes ... but gradually I learned how to avoid mistakes and how to make a score ... how to get down in two from 50 metres. For the first three or four years of my golfing life, I never knew about practising on a practice range. I still think that for any young person, it's vital to be playing holes and less vital to be endlessly repeating the same shot on a practice range. If you get an hour, set yourself to play six holes and play them until you can par them.

ALL IN THE RHYTHM

A rhythmic player will always beat a jerky one, and I think all people have their own natural rhythm. It has to do with the way you walk, speak, your nervous system. If you speak fast, you'll swing fast. If you speak with a drawl, you'll have a lovely, slow swing. Look at Greg Norman and Nick Faldo. Faldo invariably would win because he is a rhythmic player while Norman is jerky. Ernie Els and Phil Mickelson are beautifully rhythmic players, but Tiger Woods isn't.

A GREAT PASTIME

Judgement is not in your fingers but in your head. It is every golfer's personal problem to master his judgements, yet I fancy none of us poor mortals will ever be more than mere toys for the whims of the devils inside us.

Some days our judgements are uncannily correct and we may well-up with pride that at last, at long, long last, we are in command. But the next day we are back where we started, three putting and hitting up short and wondering why we are so stupid.

That is one of the reasons why golf is such a great human pastime.

The Secrets of Australia's Golfing Success, published 1961

A TENDER TOUCH

A light, tender sensitive touch is worth a ton of brawn, and this you will not get lifting weights.

Interview with *The Sunday Times*, London, July, 1960

A SIMPLE TRUTH EXPOSED

Driving the ball is generally a simple, straightforward repetition of the normal full stroke and doesn't require any more judgement than merely aiming yourself straight.

The fatal error is to try to hit extra hard.

Go to the practice tee. If you hit 100 balls with your driver, and amongst them hit 20 extra hard, you'll find no more than half a dozen of those 20 are more than five yards farther than the original 80.

The Secrets of Australia's Golfing Success, published 1961

THE MASTER EYE

Everyone has a master eye and I am convinced it's advantageous to have your front eye as your master eye. If you are left-eyed and play right-handed, as did Kel Nagle, Walter Hagen, and Bobby Jones, then you have an advantage. Phil Mickelson plays left-handed, but he's right-eyed. To tell which is your master eye, line your finger up with the line of somebody's nose with both eyes open. Ask them which of your eyes they can see. That's your master eye. I always had trouble putting because I'm right-eyed and right-handed. I don't see a straight line looking to the left, but I see a straight line looking to the right. That doesn't mean you should change anything. It just means some people have an advantage.

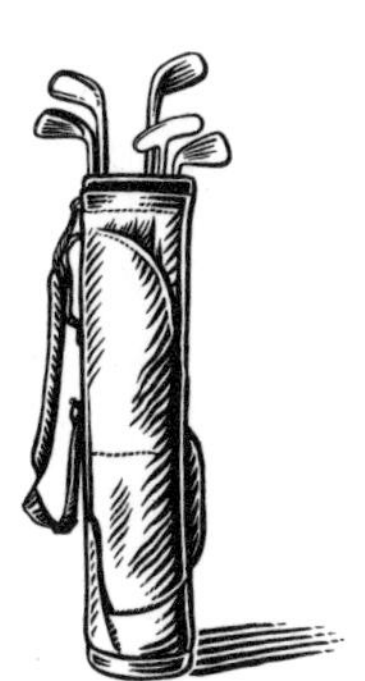

THINK ABOUT THE TARGET

Over the past 50 years, I've observed that the general view is that golf is controlled by the player's swing and this swing has to be perfected to get the perfect result. I believe the reality to be something entirely different. If you were to throw a stone into a pond, you wouldn't be thinking about where your elbow is at the point of delivery, or how much you've got to turn from the waist. You'd be thinking about the target, and if you were thinking about the target, the rest would fall into place. Even at the highest levels of golf, if you think about the target in the same way as you'd think about the pond, it will stand you in better stead than thinking about how you're going to swing. Far too many really good players today fail because they're thinking about their swing and not about where they're hitting. The great players of the '30s and '40s didn't think about their swing. They thought about getting the ball to the target. The aim should be to hit the ball at your feet to a destination, and the same should apply equally to the professional as to the social golfer.

HIT THE FAIRWAY

The main thing about golf is to get your first shot onto what used to be called fair ground, now called fairway. It doesn't matter a lot if you're 50 metres on or 50 metres back. That will be taken care of by the next shot. Getting the ball into play—or, as I call it, serving the ball into court—is vital. I first came upon this when I played the US Open in the early '50s. In those days, the US PGA made fairways we thought were ridiculously small. They were only 20 metres wide and all the players complained. It was so very different to every other tournament we played, but it became widespread. In any championship worth its salt, the targets were pretty small.

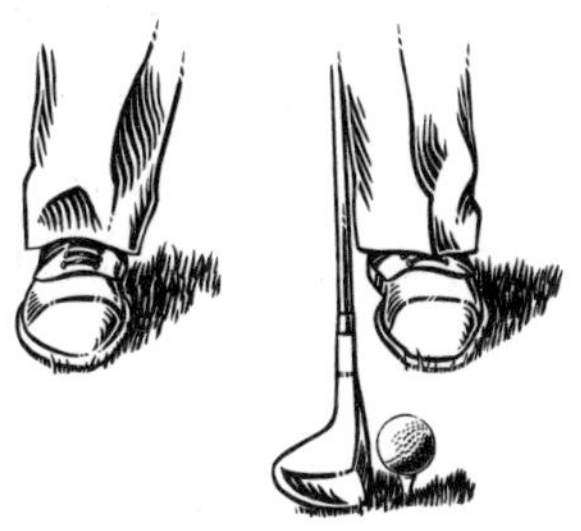

ONE STEP AT A TIME

I didn't see anybody who played well until I'd been playing for a few years. By that time I'd worked out how to get the ball from the tee to the fairway and from the fairway to the green. When I did eventually see a good player, it didn't drag me away from the line I was on. I was lucky. It's very easy to be overwhelmed watching a very good golfer. It's better to climb the ladder one step at a time and consolidate as you go. Taking a youngster to see a great player and saying "copy what they do" is poor advice. Emulating somebody means you're looking at yourself from outside. You need to look at yourself from inside. Inside your head, you'll discover what to do and you'll do it well. And, if everything is correct at address, you can't help but play well. Get your posture and your grip right and you can't go far wrong. Then it's just a matter of drawing back, turning as you go. After you've reached the zenith, you simply reverse what you've just done. If you're too upright, too bent over, have too much weight on one foot, you'll make a mess of it for sure.

SILLY ADVICE

Too many people absorb weird theories such as keeping your left arm straight or the foolish notion that you must keep your head down. That's what stops them hitting better. It's also silly to say "keep your head still". If you keep your head still, you'll hit a poor shot. Your head has to rotate and move and your face has to turn with your shot to eventually face the target. And it's almost physically impossible to keep your left arm straight. If you can't, it doesn't mean you can't play golf.

LOOK AND LEARN

I learned something from everybody, even the bad players, because if you observe them closely, you can see exactly what they do wrong.

VIDEO NASTIES

I've never analysed my own golf swing. I did see it once, on a movie, and it shocked me so much I never looked at it again. I'm sure that watching their swings on videos stops a lot of today's very talented young players from doing better. They might be able to achieve swing perfection, which enables them to hit 50 balls into a bucket with a driver, but they can't break 77. I never tried to hit 50 balls into a bucket.

A PRICELESS ASSET

What do I like about my own swing? I don't know. It's the only one I've got and I'm stuck with it. The only changes have been caused by age, as I can't swing as far back. If you only get half-cocked at the top of the swing, you play half-cocked golf. When you're young, you swing past the horizontal, which is foolishly called "over-swinging". It's not. It's a priceless asset to swing past the horizontal without any effort.

A WALKING GAME

Anyone who can walk can play golf. It is a walking game. To be a good golfer you must be a good walker. You must condition your legs.

The Sunday Times, London, July, 1960

WALK THE WALK

Let me tell you here and now that if you get tired during your round of golf you will not play your best and not win. Golf is a walking game and always will be unless America conquers the world, in which case we will all ride around courses on scooters and electric carts and invalids will win tournaments. All the good golfers you will ever see are good walkers. You do not have to outwalk a good player to beat him, but at least you have to keep up and a good pair of legs is necessary.

Walk with a steady, relaxed rhythm with the arms swinging, and you will find it will help your game of golf. The speed of your stride finds its way into your swing. If you rush between your tee shot and second, you will be inclined to rush your next swing.

The Secrets of Australia's Golfing Success, published 1961

WARMING TO THE TASK

In my day, it was enough to warm up for a day's play by hitting a dozen wedge shots. I didn't know of anybody at that time hitting a driver. The warm-up was simply to get muscles moving and your grip at the right tension.

FIT FOR GOLF

Sam Snead never went anywhere near a gymnasium. Somebody started it and it became infectious and now most professionals think that, if they don't do it, they can't win.

It's like practising. In my time, Ben Hogan started practising. He was seen hitting a pyramid of golf balls down the practice fairway and then winning. Younger players saw this and suddenly, everybody's hitting practice balls. Prior to the 1950s, nobody spent any time practising because they didn't see it to be of any benefit. Byron Nelson never hit a practice shot.

I never went to a gym. I always felt the best practice was to play golf.

There was an American golfer named Frank Stranahan. He was the heir to the Champion Sparkplugs fortune, so he had nothing else to do but play golf and lift weights. He even used to tour with his weights and you'd see him in his hotel lifting weights.

He nearly won the Open in 1947, but he went backwards, so by the mid 1950s, he was coming 50th. He proved that winning golf events had nothing to do with lifting weights.

PREPARING TO PLAY

I didn't have a set routine before playing. I'd plan my day the night before, perhaps over dinner. If I had an afternoon hit-off, I'd just sit quietly, conserve the energy. Sometimes I'd go to the course and watch ... stand around the 9th green for example. I wouldn't walk too far. It's amazing what you learn by watching other people ... watch their errors.

DEVELOP YOUR OWN STYLE

No two players are the same, although today, they're all trying to play like someone else.

FULL SET, FULL WEIGHT

If you're starting out and you don't have a full set of clubs, don't feel deprived. You're learning skills that people with full sets are not learning. I didn't have a full set for a long time. I think I got a two-wood first, then a couple of fairway irons, a pitching club and a putter. These days, I carry a driver and a strong fairway club—a 3.5-metal. I don't need anything then until a four-iron. Four, five, six, seven, eight then a sand iron-cum-pitching wedge, and a putter. I leave out clubs because it makes a big difference to your energy towards the end of your round if you're carrying, or even pulling, a heavy load.

BEST CLUBS

The two key clubs in my bag were the driver and the putter. If you could get a good pair of those you could win anything. I had to borrow some irons from John Letters in 1954 before I won at Birkdale. I had a disgusting set of irons from America which I thought might be the winning clubs but they were dreadful. The night before the championship I got these strange clubs and I played with them. After I had finished I gave them back and thanked John. I never saw them again.

National Club Golfer, 2014

LOOKING FOR LOFT

I'd never heard of a wedge until I was 21 or 22. It hadn't been invented, although it was similar to the old nine-iron I used. And, of course, there were Niblicks, all-purpose iron clubs with the loft of a modern day nine-iron. Then wedges got thrust upon us and they weren't all that useful, to be honest. If I had to play with five clubs, I wouldn't include a wedge. A seven or eight-iron would be the club to give you the most loft.

CHATTER CAN MATTER

Gamesmanship in golf is usually subtle, but if you don't have the brains to shut your eyes and ears when you're playing seriously, then you deserve what you get. Doug Bachli was a very talkative fellow and would talk the whole way. I learned from another fellow that, if you wanted to beat him, you just didn't talk to him. If he was forced to play a round without chatter, he didn't play well.

LOOK THE PART

I remember Norman von Nida showing me, in his room in Aarons Hotel, Sydney, a wardrobe so full of slacks of all colours that you couldn't see past them. I am sure he had more slacks at that time than any department store. "You've got to dress so that people know you are better than everyone else," he said. "It's good for you and it's bad for the people you play against." That was the first of many lessons in the art of climbing up the ladder. He even took me to the barber's shop to make sure my hair was cut properly, and told me never to wear a hat. "A head of hair like yours will be priceless where you're going," he said.

The Herald, Melbourne, 1964

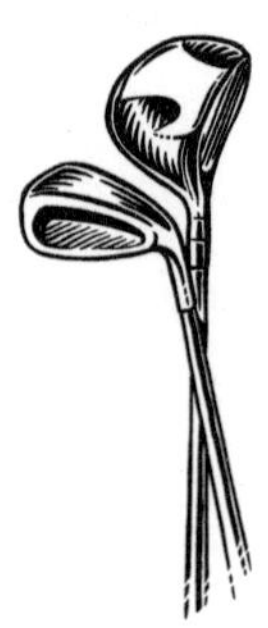

A LIVELY FAILURE

Before the Von came into my life, I'd been working as a rubber technologist for the Spalding Company at Sunshine in the Western suburbs of Melbourne. In that job, I did routine tests on golf balls, tennis balls and golf clubs, and I learned all there was to know about making golf balls. For the company, I was able to experiment. I made balls lighter. I made balls heavier. I made balls larger and smaller. I found that golf balls, at a set weight, perform much the same whether they have a silicone centre or a liquid centre or even a strawberry jam centre. At this time, I used to make my own personal golf balls, injecting a few drops of fluid into the centre of the ball with a hypodermic needle. The idea, which was patented, was to increase the internal tension and add to the weight. I thought I had made the perfect golf ball. It had all the attributes I liked. But there was one snag. The injection created a weak spot which invariably burst under extreme tension. The idea was a failure, but it certainly enlivened the ball.

The Herald, Melbourne, 1964

MY PENNANT DEBUT

In 1946, when I was 16, I was able to join Victoria Golf Club as a junior member. On my first pennant match I felt as tense as I later did in my first British Open. I played Jack Campbell, of Commonwealth, who is still one of my staunchest supporters. I won at the 19th and it all happened in such a juvenile whirl that I can't remember much about it.

The Herald, Melbourne, 1964

TURNING PROFESSIONAL

It was a run of sensational scores that turned me towards the professional ranks. In successive weeks, I scored 64 at Croydon, 63 at Northern and won as an amateur the Open 36-hole event at Victoria Golf Club with a score of 142. The next week, I went to Sydney for Australia's biggest tournament and, finishing third, I decided that golf was better than life in the factory.

The Herald, Melbourne, 1964

CONTINUE IN RAIN

At the 1948 Australian Amateur Championship at Metropolitan, rain flooded the greens, but nobody was permitted to stop. If you couldn't putt, you had to chip. During the tournament, I played Sydney doctor Jim Prendergast. On the green, we had to chip with an eight iron, and it was relatively easy as it turned out. Ten years later, I was playing with some professionals who refused to proceed because the greens were flooded. Eventually the authorities decided that, once it was flooded, play was stopped. Professional golfers are completely against increasing the "chance factor", but I firmly believe that if it's just ordinary rain, the game should continue.

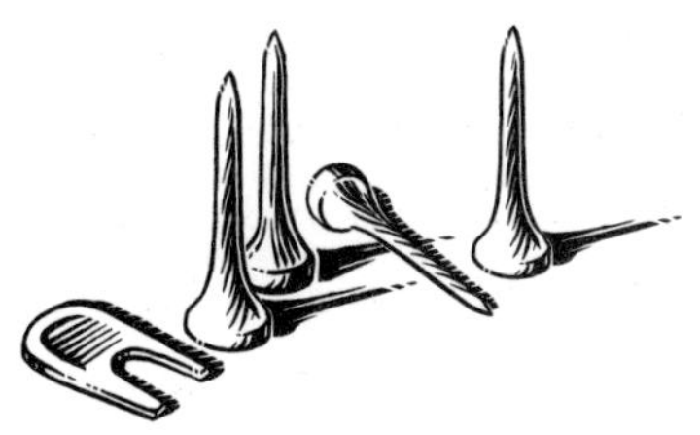

SLOW GREENS

Observing professional golf, I've noted that slow greens are more difficult to putt on. How often do you hear players complain about slow greens, saying they couldn't get the ball up to the hole. And if slow greens are a problem to deal with, then that's what we should have when there's a championship. The R&A (Royal & Ancient) has a marvellous film that runs for about 90 minutes showing Open winners from the early 20th century—Harry Vardon, James Braid, James Taylor and, after them, Walter Hagen and Gene Sarazen, and Reg Whitcombe and Henry Cotton—and it's most noticeable that the greens were like lawns. To move the ball six or seven metres, you really had to give it a bit of a whack. One-putts were unheard of and getting it to the hole was an accomplishment. Is that such a bad thing? In the future, we may get around to having championships where the greens have different speeds.

READING THE GRASS

Reading the green in my youth was about reading the speed, not the slope. Any fool can see slope. What you can't see is speed, and speed is determined by grass. You had to examine the grass to see whether the grain went with you towards the cup, or against you. Reading the grass was a skill ... one that's gone from the game. Ben Hogan, who rarely opened his mouth, was sitting in the locker room after one day's golf and said: "Anyone can putt on fast greens." It was a short sentence, but that was about all you got out of him.

HOGAN, THE QUIET MAN

I got to like Ben Hogan. I was paired with him a lot because I was the perennial British Open champion and he was winning the US Open. He was extremely courteous and, for example, when it was not his shot, he got off the stage. Other illustrious players wouldn't leave the stage. They would get in your way visually, but he didn't.

PERFECTION APPLIES

Ben Hogan could go a whole tournament, that's four rounds, without mis-hitting once. I've seen him do it. He was quite a contrast with Arnold Palmer, who could hardly go three holes without hitting one sideways or out into the trees or the rough.

The precision of Hogan's striking was incredible. I don't believe anybody has approached that, not even Nicklaus. I don't think Jack achieved that special refinement.

One never knew really what was in Hogan's mind because he never showed any indication, but he was certainly a very deep thinker. I've learned in my life that people who keep their mouth shut are judged to be a lot wiser than they really are. Hogan knew when to keep his mouth shut.

Golf Digest, 1994

TIGER'S WEAKNESSES

Tiger Woods is the only player I know who starts his swing from a static, rigid position. Everybody who has ever played well started their swing from a forward press or a waggling of the club. Tiger starts rigid and very often snatches the club away. He's what the Americans would call a slugger. He's not rhythmic. His tremendous strength has been the number of longs putts he can hole. In latter times, his putting hasn't been as successful and that has exposed weaknesses in the rest of his game, and the weakness comes from believing you can start a swing by flicking a switch. But I expect Tiger to figure it out. He has a brilliant mind and he'll figure it out eventually.

VON NIDA BLAZED THE TRAIL

Norman von Nida was the trailblazer for Australian golfers playing overseas. He went to Britain in 1946, immediately after World War II when the only way to get there was via a converted Lancaster flown by British Airways. He was wonderful for me and taught me that every player has his weaknesses. Bobby Locke did, Sam Snead did ... I recognised that I was never a really good putter, so I putted very carefully ... gently ... and got around in an average of about 34 putts. Kel Nagle was going around in 30 putts while poor old Von had the putting torments all his life and was averaging more like 36. I got very good at iron play. I wasn't a long driver so I didn't try to hit it a long way. If I sacrificed a bit of length, I was able to keep the ball on the fairway and then reliably hit the next one on the green. In those days, balls didn't fly as far but holes weren't as long, so I could handle that.

ANGER GETS YOU IN TROUBLE

I used to deal with anger on the golf course pretty quickly. From my childhood, I recognised that anger got you into trouble. There's a penalty for being angry and it's not worth the penalty in life as in golf. Anger on the golf course stems from your own deficiencies. You make a mess of things and you curse yourself. It's wise to get rid of it quickly. When I was a cranky, undisciplined teenager, I would slam clubs. I imagine everyone does that at some point. But almost immediately after I tossed a club away or cursed, I felt in myself that I'd done something stupid and that I'd made a fool of myself, so I resolved not to do it again.

AT THE FEET OF CHAMPIONS

My first overseas event was in Manila in 1950. Norman von Nida engineered an invitation for me. I had just turned professional and it was a big thing for me to play abroad, but the Von was my shepherd, so we went for a couple of weeks, travelling via Singapore, which gave me a taste for the exotic East. I did fairly well in the Philippines Open and finished about sixth. I took away quite a big prize. With what I won, I invested in a ticket to the US in January and Jim Ferrier got me an invitation to play in the Bing Crosby tournament on the Monterey Peninsula and again the following week in the Los Angeles Open.

While in America, I played only once more, in Phoenix, but it was enough to give me a taste and helped me decide what to aim for and the standard required. I'd stood at the feet of Sam Snead and Byron Nelson, and it was an inspiration for me. I actually played two rounds with Nelson in the Bing Crosby. I'd seen his black-and-white illustrated book on how to play golf, but the impression I got from the book was nothing like the reality. When I returned, I set myself to get to Britain. I had some trouble with my entry to the PGA of Australia, without which I couldn't play in Britain. There was quite an obstruction and I didn't know who could sort it out. The problem was that there was an apprenticeship scheme in place. I was lucky enough to be invited by George Naismith at Riversdale Golf Club, in Melbourne's eastern suburbs, to be one of his assistant pros. It was expected by the older members in the PGA that you were bound to the bench and that if the pro let you play on Friday afternoon, you were pretty lucky. George was more than generous and encouraged me to play a lot. He didn't like being stuck in the pro shop, so he'd go down and teach for a week in Gippsland and Warrnambool, and he took me with him. This publicised absence from Riversdale irritated some of the old pros, who reckoned I wasn't doing a proper apprenticeship.

Anyway, in the nick of time, my entry was granted and away I went, chasing after von Nida, Kel Nagle and Eric Cremin, who'd somehow got a fund together up in Sydney to take them off to play the British circuit.

LEARNING WITH LOCKE

By the end of my first visit to Britain I'd done quite well. I'd finished sixth in the Open at Portrush in Northern Ireland, now Royal Portrush, and almost won a tournament in Yorkshire. I just got pipped in the end but I won a good money prize, so I came home with a wad of notes.

At that time, Bobby Locke, who was the leading player in Britain, invited me to go to South Africa in the summer of 1951-52. This was marvellous for someone as young as me. By this time, he'd won the Open Championship twice and was one of the gods of the game. He took me in—he was between marriages, so there was ample time—and we played 63 rounds of golf, head-to-head, in nine weeks. I tried desperately to beat him and he tried desperately to beat me. He won about the first 11 times, but I worked out that I was trying too hard ... getting myself into a knot. I decided to go out gently and see what happened—and the miracle occurred. Right at the end of the match, Locke made a serious mistake instead of me making a serious mistake and I won. From there on, it was a pretty even contest. I'd learned that you get tight constantly striving for the perfect shot when there are times when you don't have to strive for perfection. If you hit the centre of the green with your iron shot, you're never far from the flag, no matter where they put it. But if you try to hit stone-dead shots all the time, you'll get caught and crash.

HERALD & WEEKLY TIMES

Me at about 15, with a club from one of my first sets, Kro-Flite, made by Spalding. Notice my grip and a loose left hand, typical in those days.

With Norman von Nida. 'You've got to dress so people know you are better than everyone else,' von Nida told me.

Top: On the eve of my first trip to Britain in 1951.

Left: This photo was taken in Singapore in 1949 by Singaporean millionaire, photographer and film-industry benefactor, Loke Wan Tho. He was tragically killed in a plane crash in Taipei in 1964.

Thomson's first Australian win as Golf pro.

By JOHN DEAN

PETER THOMSON had his first Australian professional win in the Victorian Close Golf Championship at Commonwealth on Saturday.

Thomson's rounds of 73, 71, 71, 73 — for an eight - under-standard-scratch 288 — left him eight strokes ahead of defending champion Ossie Pickworth, whose final rounds of 78 and 77 were among his worst for some years.

TOP: A newspaper clipping recording my first tournament win as a professional—the Victorian Close Golf Championship at Melbourne's Commonwealth course in 1949.

LEFT: Driving from the first tee against Ossie Pickworth around 1950.

A favourite photo of mine, with Australian tennis stars Ken McGregor and Frank Sedgman (right), taken in 1951 at the Metropolitan Golf Club during the Australian Open, which I won.

FROM THE COLLECTION OF THE METROPOLITAN GOLF CLUB, MELBOURNE.

TOP: Putting my way to victory in my first Australian Open win at Melbourne's Metropolitan course in 1951.

RIGHT: Norman von Nida during the 1952 Australian Open at Lake Karrinyup in Western Australia. Von Nida was the trailblazer for Australian golfers playing overseas.

BOTTOM: One of a series of articles on playing golf that I wrote with the fine English sports writer Henry Longhurst for Britain's *The Sunday Times*.

THE SUNDAY TIMES

THE 'EASY' WAY TO GOLF WITH PETER THOMSON—2

How to play short irons

Playing out of a Melbourne bunker in the early '50s.

At a farewell dinner with family and friends in 1951 before going to England. My father, Arthur, is on my right; my mother, Grace, is on my left.

A taste of American automobile luxury. I was playing on the US tour in 1954. Unfortunately, it wasn't my car. The book in my hand is *Golf with the Masters*, by Dave Camerer, a New York sports writer.

HERALD & WEEKLY TIMES

Waiting to putt at Melbourne's Woodlands course in the early '50s. Note the collar and tie—and I've always liked cardigans.

GETTY IMAGES

Holding the trophy aloft after winning my first British Open at Royal Birkdale in 1954. The last round was played over 36 holes. I had to make a dash back to my hotel to get an appropriate jacket for the presentation.

BOTTOM LEFT: I wasn't a great bunker player, so when I played a successful bunker shot at the 16th to help set up my first Open win at Royal Birkdale in 1954, it was deemed worthy of a headline. Note that Norman von Nida was the author of this article.

BOTTOM RIGHT: A newspaper clipping about my second British Open victory at St Andrews.

'WIZARD' SHOT WON THE OPEN

From NORMAN VON NIDA, special to The Sun

LONDON, Sun. — Melbourne's Peter Thomson played one of the most astonishing shots in the history of golf to win the British Open championship.

Thomson's stroke out of a bunker at the 16th hole was the most discussed shot in the entire tournament.

Season's last of Lowther

BRAWL AT BIG RUGBY REFEREE WALKS OFF

4 Daily Telegraph & Morning Post, Sat., July 9, 1955

THOMSON'S SECOND OPEN BREAKS JONES'S RECORD

Mechanical Golf for 281: Fallon Two More: Jowle Third

From LEONARD CRAWLEY

ST. ANDREWS, Friday.

PETER THOMSON, of Australia, won the Open Championship here this evening for the second year in succession. His score of 281 is a record for the Old Course, beating R. T. Jones's 285 here in 1927.

Thomson's four rounds were 71, 68, 70 and 72 and at once a model of consistency. He is a wonderful player in this country and in the last few years has shown us that he can take all courses in his mechanical stride.

Match and medal play come alike to him; only 10 months ago he won the Match-Play Championship here against J. Fallon, whom he beat at the 38th hole. This was after Thomson had won a memorable Open at Royal Birkdale.

Before that, he had been twice ...

How they finished

281—P. W. Thomson (Australia) 71 68 70 72
283—J. Fallon (Huddersfield) 73 67 73 70
284—F. Jowle (Edgbaston) 70 71 69 74
285—A. D. Locke (South ...

HAPPY CHAMPION.—Peter Thomson, the Australian, who retained his Open Golf Championship yesterday. His 281 is a record for the championship at St. Andrews, and is the second best ever.

One of my favourite photos of Deirdre, born two months before my first Open win at Royal Birkdale.

Thomson's Win in Open Caps Great Golf Year

By Don Lawrence

Two incidents, one the inquiring mind of a 12-year-old boy and the other a lucky marble in Tattersall's consultation, are behind the British Open golf success of Australia's two golfing Peters—Thomson and Toogood.

On Friday, Thomson became the first Australian to win the British open championship, and Toogood, overlooked for the official amateur touring team, finished first amateur in the open.

Thomson, with a fourth round of 71, for a total of 283, beat Bobby Locke, Dai Rees and Syd Scott by one stroke.

Peter Toogood's score was 291.

Their efforts capped the greatest year in Australia's golfing history.

Five Feats

In order, I would rate the five most important successes of the Australians this way:—

- Thomson's open win.
- Bachli's British amateur title.
- Toogood's finishing top amateur in open.
- Bachli's defeat of English star Ronnie White in the Inter-Dominion series.
- Australia's win in the Inter-Dominion series.

One leading golf administrator said yesterday: "It is hard to believe that our players have made such a clean sweep of the British season."

Thomson started his golf career as a lad of 12 years when he unconsciously moulded the basis of his present sound swing along the lines of veteran professional Jimmy Grace, whom he watched at Royal Park.

Grace's style was indelibly marked in Peter's sub-conscious mind and it is among the factors which have rocketed him to the pinnacle of world golf.

Both Thomson and Bachli were members of the Victoria Golf Club until Peter turned professional in 1949.

He took this step on the advice of his close friend, Harry Young, who sought Norman von Nida's advice first.

Behind the scenes these two men have done more for Thomson than anyone else.

He completed a two-year apprenticeship with Riversdale professional George Naismith before being admitted to the P.G.A.

Thomson's entry into the P.G.A. was not unanimously popular among Victoria's professionals, who thought he was getting in "under false pretences."

Unlike other assistants, Peter was not interested in bench work and even went to America while serving his apprenticeship.

Thomson has had many critics.

There was a hint of bitterness and jealousy about one "slow play" incident in Sydney two years ago, but Thomson has stood rock-like against his critics.

Toogood, a member of a famous Australian golfing family, is in England with his parents on holiday. His mother won £25,000 in a Tattersall's sweep last year.

He was the only Australian amateur to qualify.

Behind him in the open were such top amateur competitors as playboy American Frank "Muscles" Stranahan.

Sarno Proves "Weak Reed"

By Ensign

F. W. Hoysted-trained Sarno proved a "weak reed" after being backed to favoritism for the [illegible] and two-year-old mile at Flemington on Saturday.

Sarno firmed to 5-2 to displace the early favorite, Baroda Beam.

But Baroda Beam scored easily and Sarno finished 10th.

It was an excellent staying performance by Baroda Beam, who had 8.12.

Handy Position

After winning the start, Vic Hartney dropped Baroda Beam into fourth position and held him there to the turn.

Once into the straight, the colt easily raced to the front to lead by about three lengths.

Although he had the race safely won a furlong out, Hartney drove him hard right to the line.

Rose Down in Tennis Final

LONDON, July 11 (A.A.P.)

Hugh Stewart (U.S.) beat Mervyn Rose in a five-set match to win the men's singles event in the Irish Lawn Tennis championships in Dublin yesterday.

Stewart won 3-6, 6-4, 6-4, 11-13, 6-4.

Note the byline. Don Lawrence was one of Australia's finest golf writers and the man who nicknamed Jack Nicklaus 'The Golden Bear'.

Holding the trophy after winning the Open at Hoylake in 1956. I had to borrow the jacket I'm wearing from a friend, Max Shaw. Some months later he found my winner's cheque in the pocket.

OPEN CHAMPIONSHIP 1958

ROYAL LYTHAM AND ST. ANNE'S

MON DAY PLAYER P.W. THOMPSON

Hole No.	Score for Hole	Hole No.	Score for Hole
1	3	10	3
2	4	11	4
3	4	12	2
4	3	13	3
5	2	14	4
6	4	15	4
7	5	16	4
8	3	17	4
9	3	18	4
TOTAL OUT	31	TOTAL IN	32
		TOTAL OUT	31
MATCH No. 21			63

PLAYER'S SIGNATURE

MARKER'S SIGNATURE Cooper

TOP: In Melbourne in 1959 at the Canada Cup, with Governor Sir Dallas Brooks, Frank Pate, chairman of the Canada Cup, and Prime Minister Robert Menzies.

RIGHT: My card for the 1958 British Open championship qualifying round. Note the incorrect spelling of my name. I won the Open that year with rounds of 66, 72, 67 and 73.

BACK IN BRITAIN

My second trip to Britain was in April 1952, as a married man. I did pretty well, finishing second in the Open to Bobby Locke and being well up in nearly every event I played in, so again I went home with a bit of money.

FEAR MEANS FAILURE

You can get yourself into a terrible mess if you expect to hole putts and then don't. It destroys your confidence and you get irritable, cranky, reckless and stupid. The main thing for someone like me was to make sure I got two putts. Occasionally, you fluke one. Philosophically, I worked out that it's better to hope you hole a putt than to fear you're going to miss one. Even a short one. If you're fearful, you'll miss. If you say: "Well, I hope I hole this"... that's a better attitude. The reality is that everybody misses short putts, so don't let it destroy you. People who resort to different putting grips and long shafts are defeated.

GRIP CAN BE THE PROBLEM

In themselves, long-shafted putters aren't the problem; it's the grip. The articulation of the left wrist, which is upside down, isn't part of the golf stroke. You can't tee off like that, or chip like that. To use it to putt really isn't playing golf. I'm not condemning the long putter, but rather the way it's handled. And I don't understand how you can have admiration for somebody who's resorting to subterfuge. They're not the complete golfer, so they don't rate high in my estimation.

ENVYING LOCKE'S PUTTER

I can't recall too much about my first round in a British Open. It would have been at Royal Portrush in 1951 and I was using a set of irons made for me in Sydney by the East Brothers with Jim Ferrier's name on them. I forget which woods I had, but I suspect I acquired some American MacGregor woods, which were the best at the time. I used MacGregor woods when I played a series of exhibition matches against Bobby Locke and he wanted my three-wood. I used it pretty well, and when he had a hit with it, he found he also hit it pretty well. He wanted it. I said: "Well, you give me your putter", because he had this wonderful old putter he'd used all his life ... he'd had it from childhood until the day he retired. We had a stand-off for a while about this and then he did something very clever ... he had a replica of the putter made ... hickory shaft, same head, same leather grip. We made the deal and I took the putter and used it for several years, but never as well as he did. It resides now at Melbourne's Riversdale Golf Club in the showcase.

CLIMBING INTO PROSPERITY

My goal as a young player was to keep my head above water and accumulate some assets ... climb into prosperity by doing something I enjoyed doing. I have to laugh at the billionaires of today saying they're not playing this event for the money. But it's a nice feeling to have the money rolling in every week, I tell you.

LOVING THE MOMENT

You will think best when you are happiest. If you are at peace with your environment you are master and nothing baffles you. It is a good idea to make up your mind to like a course you are about to play, to like the people you are playing with and to enjoy the weather, cold or hot. Go about things with a smile on your face. Look as if you are enjoying it.

Overcome yourself and you will overcome everyone else. Be grateful that you are out there playing.

The Secrets of Australia's Golfing Success, published 1961

LOCKE THE LEGEND

Bobby Locke was a fabulous character, his life a fable. I met his aged mother and father and had Christmas dinner with them in 1952. He had his 21st birthday in New Zealand in 1938, so he was a lot older than me.

He spent four years flying with the South African Air Force during World War II and these were, I suppose, his prime years as a golfer. It was a similar story with Henry Cotton, Tommy Bolt and a lot of others. Locke returned to golf after the war and his experience in combat stiffened him so that he became such a very fierce, mean character on the course that he didn't enjoy any popularity with his fellow players. He almost went out of his way to irritate them and, at the end of his life, wasn't much mourned.

Also, if we look into the annals of the game, he doesn't feature as prominently as he should have. Nevertheless, he was a hell of a good player with his own distinct style. He played bare-handed, always played sensibly, and was a good putter, although not with the brilliance of more recent players. For example, Gary Player, who came behind him, holed 10 times as many putts as Locke ever did. As for Arnold Palmer, nobody holed long putts like he did. In Locke's time, it was thought ridiculous to try to hole a three-metre putt as the greens simply weren't as good, so the aim was to get it near enough to the hole to make the next putt a certainty. Locke always left his first putt dead by the hole, so therefore had a reputation for being a good putter.

THE LOCKE DRAMA OF '57

My relationship with Bobby Locke had a sad ending. I had won the 1954 and '55 British Opens, so we had won two each. I organised a series of matches in Australia and New Zealand and he was guaranteed quite a bit of money. Then, just after I won the 1956 British Open, he casually told me he wasn't coming to Australia. I thought I'd offended him, but he said he was too old, even though he was only 40 years. So we had to cancel his tour and he seemed stand-offish.

Then, in the '57 British Open, something happened which destroyed our friendship altogether. On the final green at St Andrews, Locke, who was playing ahead of me by about five holes, hit his second shot three or four metres from the hole and marked it. He was playing with Bruce Crampton, who asked him to move his marker because it was on the line of his putt. Locke moved it, but in the meantime realised he was about to achieve something he had never expected to do—win the Open for the third time. When the time came to putt, he forgot to move the marker back to its original spot. He took two putts, doffed his cap and away we went. Whether he realised later what he'd done, we'll never know, but somebody rang the R&A to say Locke hadn't used his putter to restore the marker to its correct position. He defeated me by four strokes and because there was no justification for any penalty or disqualification, the result stood.

I had no knowledge of what had happened. I stood with Locke at the presentation while he had a photograph taken of him holding the cup, and I was thinking we might be able to get together again in Australia. Within a week or so, the story got out about his putt, but I don't know from where it originated. Henry Cotton was making a noise, and then Norman von Nida got into the act by stating publicly that Locke should have been disqualified. There was no provision for a penalty under the rules as they then were, so the penalty had to be disqualification. Von Nida made the point that I should have been the winner, and he's still saying it today. That didn't do me any good.

Locke and I didn't cross paths for years ... but he was very contemptuous of me, very angry. But I can honestly say that the storm wasn't my doing. It was all very sad, because all his life Locke had been very meticulous on the golf course. He dressed immaculately, in business shirt and tie. If it got hot, he removed the tie, although this didn't happen very often in Britain. I think that the realisation he had made this terrible mistake in etiquette destroyed him and he took to drinking. He was a beer drinker and he started drinking a lot of it.

One day towards the end of the '50s, he was driving away from the golf club in Cape Town, came to a level crossing and waited for a train to pass. When it passed, he went to cross, but a train from the other direction smashed into his car, crushing his skull and smashing an eye. It took him a couple of years to recover, but he was never the same again. I saw him again in the '80s when I was in Johannesburg to play a seniors tournament. His wife was very keen that I should talk to him, so I did, but he wasn't the man he used to be, as his mind drifted. It was all very sad.

FREE AS A BIRD

When I went to Britain to play, I was competing against much older golfers. I was in my early 20s and all the famous players—Dai Rees, Charlie Ward, Dick Burton, Alf Pagham, Reg Whitcombe, Henry Cotton—were 10 or 15 years older. And they were all club professionals. Henry Cotton said to me: "Are you really serious in believing you can make a living out of playing tournaments, because I think it's impossible?"

Cotton, throughout his career, was never without a club job and died in one, in Portugal. And this was the case with everyone else, except Norman von Nida, whose first club job came when he was 60. Even the Americans—Ben Hogan, Sam Snead—were never without club jobs. But here's me, as free as a bird, playing golf and not having to worry about a pro shop. At the time, we'd play Wednesday, Thursday and two rounds on Friday. Then all the blokes would drive home because, on Saturday mornings, they had to be in their shop. It was an advantage for me that I didn't have such obligations, and that should be remembered.

A GENTLE TEACHER

I am a good teacher of top standard players, but not much good at teaching beginners. I could help a lot of today's top players, including Tiger Woods, although he wouldn't turn to me for advice. It's obvious what's wrong with him—he grips too tight and he's too rigid. However, I think it's too late for him to change. I also enjoy helping people to play better and I do this for my friends and my wife; while I refuse to mess with the playing style of children. Let them do it their way and just gently straighten them up. There are things you must do, and things you must not do ... children do it naturally and you build on this. That's how you make good golfers out of kids.

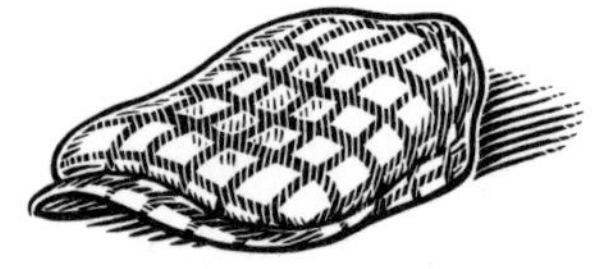

FEELING THE SHOT

In 2004, Melbourne photographer Kim Baker asked me if I had any suggested locations for a photo at Royal Birkdale to mark 50 years since my first British Open. We went to a par three on the back nine where, in the final round of the Open, I had hit a four-iron from the tee. I hit it with a slow swing and kept the blade a little open because there was a strong right-to-left wind. The ball flew beautifully, slicing a little into the wind, which held it straight. It finished a yard from the hole, but I missed the putt. I was playing against Tony Lema. There were two rounds in the day. He'd done well in the morning, but by the afternoon he was tired. He wasn't used to walking that far in a day. I went around in 71 for the last round with 35 putts, so I didn't miss-hit one shot in the afternoon. Not one. Baker asked me if, 50 years after my first British Open, I could still see the shot in my mind. "Still see it? I can still feel it," I told him. And I still can.

CLOSE YOUR MIND

My preparation for a round centred on feel ... the feel of the club, the feel of the grip. Before an important championship, I wound on new leather grips because the leather used to deteriorate badly and lose its tackiness and softness. It was a big problem we had then ... to keep grips feeling right. A couple of days before, I'd give the assistant in the pro shop £5 to wrap some new grips for me, while I tried to keep my mind closed to all outside interferences.

During the tournament, I'd know where I was on the scoreboard, but the best thing is not to know other people's problems or progress. In the end, you can't do much about it. You just try to play your best. If you know what you're doing, you have no fear of making mistakes. People who don't know what they're doing, who instinctively feel that they might fall over at the next step, invariably do so. Once a carpenter has mastered all his tools, he can make anything.

BEATING THE BEST

If you are playing an opponent who's in very good form, who's hitting well, you know you've got to play at that level.

Some people are difficult to play with. Ben Hogan, for instance, was very easy to play with because he didn't strut the stage. But Arnold Palmer was very difficult to play with because he wanted to be centre stage all the time, and indeed he was. Jack Nicklaus would be in the same category. I think they felt, "These people are here to see me."

When you played Nicklaus, was there ever a doubt in your mind you could win?

Oh, yes, because I recognised him as somebody very difficult to beat. He had an enormous advantage over most people in that he could hit so far. Then he sort of exuded that enormous egotism. It was very difficult to ignore him.

Was Arnold in the same category?

Yes, Arnold was in the same category, but then you always knew you had a hope, because he played enough bad shots to give you encouragement.

Golf Digest, 1994

FEAR CAN BEAT YOU

The first Australian Open I played was in 1950 at Kooyonga, Adelaide. I was still just 21 and a professional's assistant at Riversdale and, as it turned out, I very nearly won. In the last round, I went out in 30 strokes and was neck and neck with Norman von Nida. The second nine I found somewhat more difficult—36, I think—and von Nida won by one shot. I was too young and didn't have enough experience in tight situations like that. It's difficult to avoid becoming tense when you think you should win; and the very tension can beat you ... holding on too tight, a little fear creeping in. Fear is the enemy. You do all sorts of silly things when you're fearful. Pressure can be different things to different people. It can be exhilarating. It can lift you. But if you come to the moment of truth and you're quivering in your shoes, you'll fail. Sometimes in my playing life I most certainly was fearful and I invariably made a mess of things. Hope is better than fear.

MY FIRST OPEN WIN

I won the Australian Open in September 1951, on the old Metropolitan layout in Melbourne's famous sandbelt. The front nine holes are substantially intact today, but much of the course was taken over in a government acquisition for the expansion of two schools. While the club was able to purchase land near the clubhouse, it had been farmed for vegetables and was said to be too full of chemicals and fertiliser. It wasn't pure sand like the original layout.

When I played it, the course went all the way down to Centre Road ... the 14th hole and the 15th tee were actually on the boundary of Centre Road ... a long way. Anyway, in my run to the post, I played the long par four 17th with a driver and a two-iron, but I went through the green into a little pot bunker. I wasn't very good at bunker play and, in fact, kept out of them for that reason. I had a real fear of them and this was my moment of truth. Final day, 17th hole. I think I was leading, but I don't know for certain because they didn't have leaderboards in those days. However, I knew von Nida was pretty close on my heels. This bunker shot of about three metres was a splash out of the sand, and I hit it into the hole. A par up the last, and I won.

I had a nice picture taken later that day with Frank Sedgman and Ken McGregor, two tennis stars about my age who had come down to watch. I'd also made friends with some of the cricketers—Neil Harvey, whom I'd played cricket against when he was at Collingwood Technical College and I was at Brunswick Tech., and Keith Miller, this famous cricketer who regularly came to play golf at Riversdale. By the way, Keith wasn't too bad at golf ... a bit of a swashbuckler who'd send the ball in all directions.

THE IRRESISTIBLE VON NIDA

In the early 1950s, the Australian Tour didn't exist. There was the Australian Open and the PGA, neither of which had too much prizemoney—those who entered certainly didn't do so for the cash. Most professional players had club jobs and that was their bread and butter, while playing for money was the icing on the cake. Norman von Nida was making a living from playing, but he was playing exhibitions and he inspired me to follow suit. He actually took me under his wing and I'd play against him in various places where we'd earn small amounts which sometimes were as much as winning a tournament.

I found Norman irresistible. He was fiery and dogmatic; instinctively, I didn't want to be like him. I wanted to be what he was, not who he was. He was a bit of a naughty boy and I remember him once driving me in Sydney when he found the traffic so irksome that he drove around the wrong side of a tram, which I thought was an extraordinary thing to do. But that was typical of him ... a law unto himself. But he was very, very helpful to me. Had he been obstructive and nasty, I might not have had much success, so I'm grateful to him.

He was a pathfinder, playing in America as early as the 1940s, and that inspired me and, subsequently, a whole host of players—Bruce Devlin, Bruce Crampton, Frank Phillips, Billy Dunk. Norman was an all-round golfer and didn't have any big weakness, except his temper. He was very small and, in fact, I think he secretly wanted to be a jockey because he had an intense interest in horse racing. In those days we played without gloves and I noticed his beautiful hand action. However, he did have a bit of a weakness with putting and never got the hang of it. It was a bit pathetic really, and it annoyed him, with the consequence he was prone to throwing putters when they didn't do what he wanted them to do.

A SUMMER GAME

I didn't play Australian Opens much during the 1950s because the event was scheduled for August, a time once considered to be the best time of the year for a championship because the weather was rough and cold. I wasn't home from Europe or America most years in August and it wasn't until the '60s that the event was shifted to later in the year—late September and then into October—and I was able to enter. Golf was a winter game until well into the early '60s, when it became a summer game, and rightly so.

BUNKERS = PENALTY

Is there anything on a golf course more innocuous than large bunkers with a depth of two inches? They abound. Where pray, is the example they are following? Hazards, sand bunkers included, are supposedly penalty areas. There has to be a penalty for getting caught in error.

If it is a simple matter for an experienced player to hit his ball from a bunker onto the green with the same ease with which he would do if from the fairway, is it a bunker at all? I think not. And we hardly need to go to the expense of building them unless they are mere decorations. And even then they fall like some pop culture, there to be laughed at.

Peter Thomson: in his foreword in *Hazards*, published 1993

A BUNKER MENTALITY

I never wanted to be a great bunker player because I felt it was a mistake to get into a bunker in the first place. But I got a great tip from Bobby Locke, passed on to him by Sam Snead. Locke said: "You've got to swing the club long and slow. Don't hit it fiercely. Hit the sand softly." Watch somebody good at it and that's exactly what they do.

MISSING OUT

If you will tolerate one man's opinion, I will say that hazards should be laid down between you and your target, within your reach and not so enormous that the target is hidden. They should not span an area so wide that they cannot be avoided by taking the long road home, and they should not, except on rare occasions, be so punishing as to render escape impossible. People who find the flat of the fairway with their drives and the middle of greens with their approach, miss the most fascinating part of the game.

Foreword in *Hazards*, published 1993

GOLF, A LONG-LIFE SPORT

I won three Australian Opens, the first and third 21 years apart. This gives you an idea of how long a golfer's career can last. I was 21 when I won the first and 42 when I won my last. It's rare to find a sport in which you can play at the top level for that long, and that's one of the beauties of golf. I think from the age of about 55, there's a general deterioration and one of the key areas is eyesight.

PERFORMING MACHINES

I never thought in yards or metres, rather, I thought in clubs. Even today, I look ahead and see where my seven-iron will go, or my five-iron. I had a caddie for 17 years in Britain—Jackie Leigh, a good amateur player. He never once opened his mouth to tell me what club to hit. Sometimes, for conversation, I would say: "I'm going to hit a three-iron here" and he'd say: "Good." I made my own judgements and I still think it's important to be self-reliant.

Nowadays, there's an attempt to turn you into a machine. Your inner thoughts are about how you will actually hit the ball. But there's another way of thinking, which is "where am I going to hit it?" ... thinking from the target back to the ball. That's the way I played golf, and the way the people of my era played. Now, somebody else makes the decision about which club to put into your hands and all you are doing is performing like a machine. This may explain why so many of our really talented young golfers can't seem to put four rounds together.

TECHNOLOGY SHORTENS COURSES

Golf ball technology must change ... fewer and smaller dimples, so that the ball doesn't go so far. It's a sad fact that the modern ball has made courses shorter than they used to be. Even the Old Course at St Andrews has had to be stretched after more than 100 years, although it hasn't made any difference—they still shoot in the low 60s. And Royal Melbourne's composite course has had a 60 played on it by Ernie Els. Technology means that now, in my mid 70s, I can drive almost as far as in my youth, although my iron play is different as I don't have the strength I once had. With different balls, club players won't notice any change for a while, but technology might take 50 metres off Tiger Woods' drive, and five off mine.

INTEGRITY MATTERS

I respect any golf course that has integrity. The top four in Sydney are Royal Sydney, The Lakes, The Australian Golf Club and New South Wales Golf Club. Adelaide has four good ones—Kooyonga, Royal Adelaide, Glenelg and The Grange. Perth has Lake Karrinyup, Cottesloe and a few others. But Melbourne is richer than any other city in its golf courses, largely because of the legacy left by Royal Melbourne Golf Club in creating its west course, which was the inspiration of Dr Alister MacKenzie in partnership with Alex Russell. That seemed to inspire a lot of people to try and emulate what Royal Melbourne had done, thus we saw Victoria, Yarra Yarra, Metropolitan, Kingswood, Keysborough, Cranbourne, Huntingdale ... As for golf courses of integrity, I know this is an unusual word, but, to me, it means strength of features, proper dimensions, which give an obvious look of a golf course, not too many trees, but enough for the enhancement of bird life and habitat without interfering too much with the golf. Add to this a high standard of maintenance, which may well be the most important thing of all.

A CRYSTAL BALL

Golf in the next decade will probably see double the number of players, now that China is starting to show an interest. Golf courses will become more crowded and there will be more courses. But the game has endured to this point in essentially the same form as it started. That's part of its charm and I doubt that people are silly enough to destroy that. Credibility will be given to those courses that adhere to the game's traditions.

IN CHINA

I was recently on the Chinese island of Hainan, speaking to the governor, and I commented that he had a lot of golf courses on his island. "Yes," he said. "I've told the national government that I want 100 courses. I asked how many he had so far and he said "60". So golf in China is exploding, but more so in areas where there's a tolerance to golf courses taking over the land.

PLAYING ON YOUR OWN

The lure of golf to me as a kid was whacking the ball and making a score. Every time I went out to play, I had a target of getting a better score than I did the previous day. If I'd been confined to endlessly hitting balls off a mat, I doubt I would have stuck at it. I never minded spending time by myself. I never felt like I needed company. It wasn't that I was a loner, but logically, when you play golf, you're on your own and not usually part of any team. I still enjoy my own company today. I don't feel that I need to be busy with people all the time. I've learnt in my own experience that it's really important to have time to yourself, to generate your own thoughts, instead of reacting to outside stimuli. The majority of people wake up in the morning and spend their whole day reacting. For them, there may not be a time when they can get away from outside stimuli, so they don't think from inside and generate their own thoughts. Most people can't afford that luxury of time. For that reason, I was never a talker on the golf course. Certainly less of a talker than other people.

THINK ABOUT YOUR ERRORS

A good golf shot doesn't come by accident. Somehow, you've prepared, thought it out. And if you pull it off, you feel very warm inside. That's the real basis of golf.

When I was playing really well, through the 1950s, '60s and '70s, if I could get around the course with just three mis-hit shots, I knew I was playing pretty well. If I got around with just two or only one, I was playing super well. If I played a round and reckoned I'd hit six or seven really bad shots, then I'd think about it and it would worry me. I then would analyse why I made those errors. I'd think it through, not go to the practice fairway. Golf commentator Peter Alliss tells a story about me on the day before the 1955 Open at St Andrews. He saw me hitting half-shanks with my irons and slices with the driver and, when I finished, asked me if I was going to the practice fairway. "No," I said. "I'm going back to the hotel to think about it." And I won the championship. That's his story and I've heard him tell it several times.

DISCIPLINE WINS OUT

Tom Watson has done it all with his brain, which is very much to be admired. He is not an especially gifted player. Nor was I. But he is one who does supreme things by discipline, work and using his brains.

Some people can apply the discipline to one field, like playing golf, then can be an awful bastard in another direction. I am no saint and I would suspect that some of those golfers who have succeeded on the links might have been very different in their social lives—or married lives or something else. I don't suggest that somebody who shows the discipline on the links is necessarily a saint. Sometimes the discipline required is so draining that once you are away from it, there is a release.

John Daly is one of the most gifted players I have ever seen. He is in the gifted category of Seve Ballesteros and Sam Snead. Without even using his brain, he is going to be enormously effective playing golf. If you put Tom Watson's head on Daly's shoulders, you would have the greatest player of all time.

Golf Digest, 1994

THE TOP PLAYERS

I'm often asked to name the top 10 players I came upon during my playing days. There's Sam Snead, Ben Hogan, Bobby Locke, Julius Boros, Henry Cotton, and the most famous winner of all time, Jack Nicklaus. But then I include one of the most amazing players I saw, Brazilian Mario González. People wonder why I include him and regard his nomination as something of a shock.

I played with him quite a lot and I was always struck by his incredible technique. He was as thin as a drink of water and about six feet (183 centimetres) tall, with a lovely long, ultra-slow swing which was mesmerising to watch. I once played an exhibition match with him in Chicago and he birdied the first seven holes. I'd never heard of anybody doing that. His record showed that, in South America, he was absolutely unbeatable through the late 1940s, '50s and half of the '60s. He held down a club job at the Gavea Country Club in Rio de Janeiro and didn't venture too far from there. He played in the 1954 British Open as an amateur but he didn't win, which was a surprise. The poor fellow told me he was shivering the whole time because he wasn't used to the cold weather. The other South American I always include is Roberto De Vicenzo, who won the Open in 1967 and played wonderfully well into his 70s. In my seniors career, I'd have to mention Don January, along with Gene Littler, an amazing machine-like player who wasn't especially electric to watch.

As for current-day players, I find it very hard to rate them in my all-time list because the game is so much easier than it once was. For example, it's very hard to assess old Tom Morris, or young Tom

Morris, who won the Open three times in succession, because they played with very primitive clubs on very primitive links. They must have had immense talent to get the scores they did. It's difficult to compare them with Sam Snead, who played 50 years later. It's equally difficult to compare the modern players with Snead, Ben Hogan and the like.

I sometimes wonder whether the modern players had the talent some of those older players had. For instance, Morris never wore a glove and it was difficult to handle a shiny leather grip the way it had to be done. It took a lot of skill. Today, they play with a fine glove which is like a second piece of skin on the hands, the grips are helpful and the lies are always perfect. It all makes it very hard to say that the modern player, like Tiger Woods, Ernie Els and Vijay Singh, is better than Snead or Hogan.

GREAT SCOTT

I put Adam Scott's win in the 2013 US Masters up there with the greatest achievements by an Australian golfer, but I'm not sure if it's the "greatest".

You've got to think of Greg Norman winning two British Opens, along with others, but it was certainly the most spectacular of all of them. We were all hoping Adam would not slip up, especially after what had happened to him the year before at Lytham.

Those images of him holing his putt on the 72nd green, then again in the play-off, will live with us forever.

VIJAY IS HIS OWN MAN

I like Vijay Singh. He's a self-made, self-reliant golfer. He doesn't have anyone coaching him or counselling him about psychology, and I admire him for that. In fact, I only admire people who can demonstrate they use their own brains. As I watch sportsmen of all kinds ... cricketers, footballers of all codes ... the most interesting part is watching his/her brain at work. Forget the brawn or what they can do with hands and feet; I like to watch the way they think about things. So many good players are constantly looking for someone to tell them what's wrong or what to do. That's why they don't improve. They can't think for themselves.

NORMAN'S STIFF PLAY

Greg Norman is already being remembered for the events he didn't win, but his critics forget he was the top money-winner for the best part of 10 years—an amazing achievement. People tend to think he lost this championship and he should have won that championship and that he didn't perform well when the crunch was there, but that's unfair. I watched him emerge from boyhood and I feel he didn't latch onto the right techniques. He played very stiffly and hung onto the club very tightly. I think that's why he didn't win more. He gripped it like a vice, and that's entirely the wrong technique when playing at the highest level. It had nothing to do with his brain. He just had faith in the wrong things.

BAKER-FINCH'S PROBLEM

Everyone tried to help Ian Baker-Finch. The problem was that he didn't know what he was doing. He'd never built his swing from a base so he didn't know what was required to make a reliable golf shot. When something went wrong, he'd wonder what happened. For example, if you're an accountant, you have to learn the basics of accountancy. Ian hadn't built a knowledge pyramid. And it's a good thing that golf is like that. There are things you have to learn for yourself. You can't find it all in a book.

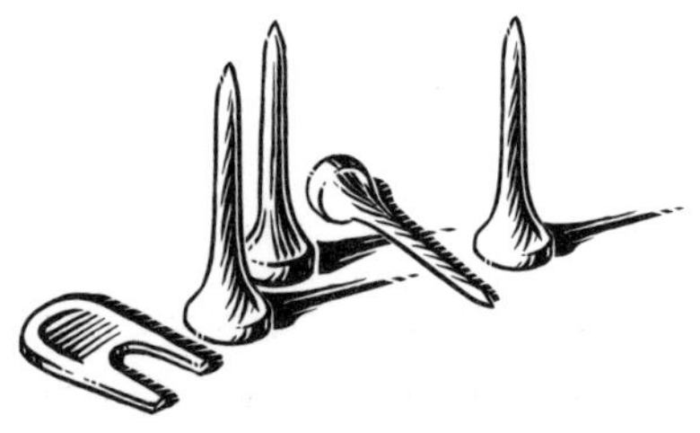

HAPPY IN THE MIDDLE

I've come to believe that, in an event with 150 players, there are only about a dozen who want to win. It's easy to settle into a field around 10th to 20th place, which doesn't require too much hard thinking or bring much strain, and still take home $10,000. Many are content with that. To get into the top two or three, that's when it's hard and if you haven't got a strong stomach, it will turn over. It's like in any organisation—a lot of people are happy with middle-level management and don't want to be a boss. That's human nature.

COMPETITIVE STREAK

I'm naturally competitive. If I can't be competitive on the golf course, I'll be competitive in other ways. For example, I want to be the world's best golf course architect and I refuse to bow to anybody. I sometimes find myself competitive on the road and have to pull myself back, get in line and wait my turn like everybody else.

THE POWER OF RANKINGS

The five golf circuits on the planet these days revolve around what is added up as rankings. This is a list that suggests who is best or where one sits on the ladder going up or down. Those who play their lives away chasing prizemoney are victims of its power. Rankings determine who gets into limited fields, where the biggest of golf's money is fought over. To pass up a tournament that has a large "pot" is a backwards career step. To pass up one with a small winner's cheque doesn't do much damage. This system has never been accepted as perfect, but like democracy, it is better than any other. After initial attempts back in the 1950s to rank tournaments, which proved too difficult, it finally and permanently came down to dollars. The leading events get bonus points so that everyone is more or less content. Ben Hogan, who strutted through the '50s, playing no more than four events a year, would not have made the list. At least he would not have made the top of the list, even had he won all four "majors".

The Age, Melbourne, December 11, 1999

THE INSUBSTANTIAL SKINS

"Skins", a form of amateur golf-gambling-turned-professional-pot-scrambling, is an inconsequential form of televised golf that tickles those who crave instant gratification, like Wheel Of Fortune and other quiz shows. Players are asked to throw caution to the wind and go all out for entertainment instead of grinding at their trade. The form bears little relationship to the real thing. The best news that will ever come out of it is for some future champion to turn his back on such appearances as beneath his, or her, dignity.

The Age, Melbourne, November 23, 2004

LEFT IS ALL RIGHT

Lefties in golf are a minority, not easily identified in the annals of the game. One needs to be fairly ancient to have heard of Harry Williams or Len Nettlefold. It was thought to be a golfing handicap until Canadian Mike Weir and American Phil Mickelson finally broke through in the Masters at Augusta in 2003 and 2004. There was an absurd era when naturally gifted teenagers were persuaded to change clubs and play right-handed if they held any ambitions. There is no earthly reason why golf cannot be played from either side of the ball. Golf courses cannot be made easier or more difficult if you play one way or the other. Simply, the golf ball doesn't know who is hitting it.

The Age, Melbourne, November 26, 2004

PROTECT TRADITION

Sporting championships that endure to be 100 years old should be held sacrosanct—protected in appropriate ways by their own particular sporting bodies—not thrown to the wolves of commercialism by allowing the game's top players to be lured away by the smell of easy money. To schedule a particularly farcical form of golf such as a "skins" game against the Australian Open championship in its centenary year is a sorry indictment of the golf's world scheduling. The US Tour should be more sympathetic to the world's real golf fans.

The Age, Melbourne, November 23, 2004

APPEARANCE FEES ARE DEMEANING

The payment of appearance fees in events that purport to be "championships", where everyone starts on an even footing, has forever been an embarrassment. The banning of it since 1953 has been the making of the US PGA Tour. Places such as Australia, Brazil and Morocco have all succumbed to the temptation to "buy" someone's appearance. It is demeaning.

The Age, Melbourne, April 27, 2001

CONSISTENT PUTTING

I've tried the Aaron Baddeley style of putting—just stepping up and hitting it. It suits some, not others, and it doesn't suit me. In Baddeley's case, it's a matter of getting your thoughts right before stepping up to hit. It's not easy to do that. And I've tried just looking at the hole, not the ball. And the ball, not the hole. But whatever you do, do the same thing all the time.

GET RID OF THE WEDGE

I got deadly with short irons because the ball went directly at the flag and didn't fly as high as they send it today. Some bright spark will ask his ball manufacturer to make a ball that doesn't go so high. They'll sacrifice some distance off the tee, but gain enormous accuracy with their short game. If you can't get your wedge near the hole, then you're not going to score well. I remember at the Heineken Classic two years ago, I came out of the clubhouse and watched them play Royal Melbourne's 18th west. From side on, I watched this fellow hit about a 100-metre wedge shot. The ball went as high as it went far. And that's the way they're all playing now. And it helps explain why they're not getting near the hole. So find a ball that doesn't fly so high or take less loft. Pitch with the nine-iron. Get rid of the wedge.

LIFTING OUR CHAMPIONSHIPS

The Australian Golf Union has recently attempted to raise the difficulty factor of the rostered Australian Open courses, to bring them nearer the venues that host the British and the US Opens. Holes have been lengthened, bunkering adjusted for the professional driving and, generally, the rough has been stimulated to cause headaches for those who can't hit straight. The result of this is to lift our championship to a higher world ranking, although not to the dizzy heights of the two world events. Royal Troon is light years ahead of any Australian venue—but at least we are somewhere in sight.

The Age, Melbourne, November 26, 1997

HOPING FOR THE UNEXPECTED

I think people watching golf want to see the unexpected, but we, too, often get the opposite ... a blast off the tee, the ball doesn't bounce more than a few metres after it lands and the next one sticks in the green like a dart in a dartboard. That's boring; not like getting a bad lie and watching them get out of the predicament they themselves got into. That gives joy to people.

LET'S PLAY THE BRITISH

What we need in Australia is an international golf event. Get the Australian flag flying and the band playing. And the first people we should take on would be the British. In a year when the British are not playing Ryder Cup, they should play Australia. Look at the interest that cricket between England and Australia generates. Never underestimate the power of national pride in these things.

WE NEED TOUGHER COURSES

To get the Australian Open recognised anywhere in the world, it must be played on a course which at least approaches the difficulty of the British and US Opens. It has never been anywhere near that and that's one reason why it's never had any recognition. Look at the list of winners ... so many were paid to come here. It's not as if they said: "Let's go play in the Australian Open." The Open gives us a chance to differentiate ourselves from Japan, Mexico, anywhere in Europe ... "Come here because we've got a difficult course." If we had five difficult courses, we could rotate it, as they do with the British Open, but we haven't yet got five.

RAKES WITH TEETH

The rake ... a simple object, but so many clubs get it wrong. Garden rakes don't do the job—they just smooth the sand. The professional comes along and he's laughing at it because he can get as near from that lie as he can from a long putt. You have to have rakes with teeth, which loosen the sand right up to the sides, where the ball lodges in the grooves. Then you get some variable lies and stances—enough to make professionals dread these bunkers. That would change their whole attitude towards firing at the green. At the moment, they don't mind firing at the green because, if they miss, they'll land in some nice bunker which somebody has raked beautifully for them.

MEETING THE SPORTS EDITOR

From 1949 to 1951, it was difficult to make a living as a pro. There was only a handful of tournaments a year and the prizes were pretty small. Norman von Nida took me around playing exhibitions for money and I was able to pick up a couple of thousand pounds. Then there was some income from Dunlop and some other bits and pieces, but I then thought about golf journalism ... that this could be a real job with a solid backing. I went into the Argus office and met sports editor Bill Cust. I submitted something, which he read and said: "Now, I want you to understand that not only golfers are going to read this. If your grandmother can't understand what you're writing, it's a lousy bit of writing." It was good advice ... make it easily understood, and I've always thought of my grandmother while I'm writing.

SPONTANEOUS WRITING

I don't like re-reading what I've written. I've found the best results are spontaneous. I used to read a lot and learn from people who could write. I try to think of a good start, then a flow, then a pointed message if I can find one. That's how I get the job done—to say something of some importance. And I try not to write about myself (except in this book, of course). I seldom use "I".

MISPLACED HYPE

We Australians are a weird mob, aren't we? We don't hype our own sportsmen and women. That's not in our make-up. We make them earn their credits, usually the hard way. Yet we are softies for someone else's champions. In the field (of the Australian Open) was "our" Tiger Woods, an Australian amateur champion by the name of David Gleeson. He also helped win the Eisenhower Trophy for us in Manila last week. He swings as well as Woods without the same dramatic power twist. He is destined for top honours, yet, in spite of playing the first two rounds with Greg Norman, nobody knew he was there. Yesterday, he finished off his first Open with a two-under 70 for a total of nine-over. It was an impressive debut. He could do with some hype, but he won't get it. Not from us. They will continue to trumpet imports and take him for granted. Maybe he will emigrate (David Gleeson is now playing on the Asian tour).

The Age, Melbourne, November 25, 1996

NORMAN'S CURIOUS PERSONALITY

Greg Norman is, as always, a curious personality, tense and edgy to start with, throwing verbal punches without too much thought, then showing a fierceness in his demonstration of his points. His golf, though, speaks for itself.

The Age, Melbourne, November 22, 1995

THE WET WEATHER BLUES

Yesterday was one of those miserably cold and uncomfortable days when a golfer playing seriously needs three caddies: one to keep the water out of the bag, one to carry the umbrella and one to keep up the dry towel supply. Golf is the only game silly enough to carry on when sensible people are indoors by the fireside.

The Age, Melbourne, November 23, 1996

RAINED OUT

Since the day in the 1960s when the United States PGA Tour decided to complete rained-off rounds on the following day, the tournament scene has been a mess. Before that, whenever rain or poor light stopped play, the day's scores were declared null and void. It was all neat and tidy. Four-round events were reduced to three and the only whingers were those who posted the best rounds of their career before time ran out. The rest had reason to be grateful. Bad weather on the US tour can go on for days, however, so events could be reduced to nothing if rain refused to let up. Thus, the practice of coming back the next morning to finish the round was introduced. The rest of the world took it up and that's where we got into a tangle.

Yesterday, the heavens wrathfully opened up on Sydney, a fairly common occurrence at this time of year, meaning the championship (the Australian Open)—and players—suffered. Play was stopped at 1.12pm because four greens were awash. Putting was not possible and the field repaired to the shelter and warmth of the clubrooms until 3pm. Tiger Woods had one important hole left unplayed. Greg Norman had played the first two and had marked his ball on the third green, without knowing whether that would be his last shot for the day. Play resumed when there was no hope of finishing the round before dark. Such an arrangement is grossly unfair to those who face a round broken by a short night's sleep with an early morning dash to where they left off. Soaked-to-the-skin officials suffer more, since their efforts are always unrewarded.

The Age, Melbourne, November 23, 1996

PICKWORTH THE PRO

I thought Ossie Pickworth was the best golfer Australia had through the 1940s and the first half of the '50s. He won just about everything he played in, and he didn't play in too much. He travelled from Australia just once, to the 1950 British Open at Royal Lytham, and although he didn't win, he won the Irish Open a couple of weeks later at Royal Dublin—and that was quite an accomplishment. He took care of most people who tried to take him on, including Jim Ferrier and myself as an up-and-comer.

I got a terrible going over from him one day at Metropolitan, 5 and 4, and he beat me in the final of another 36-hole match-play at Royal Melbourne, his home course, with a three at the last. He wasn't a very long hitter and it bothered him. He once asked me how he could hit it longer and I said: "Well, hit it harder." He was a very soft, very smooth swinger. But he could do things. He wasn't tall, but he had long legs and arms and everything moved in his swing. He had a bit of a twirl of the club over his head after he hit a shot, easily identifiable from a long way away. He also was deadly around the green. Pickworth had his own method, his own rhythm, and he repeated it perfectly each time. And he had a lot of cheek. He never bowed to anybody. He also putted like Aaron Baddeley ... just stepped over it, and bang.

Pickworth was the club pro at Royal Melbourne from 1948 onwards. It wasn't lucrative, but it was a good, solid job. He stuck to home ground because the club wouldn't have been too happy if he'd been away for long periods. He may not have made any money, anyway. He was always laughing ... had a great smile. I don't think he ever played amateur golf and grew up as an assistant pro in Sydney—Manly, I think. There was clear distinction in those days between amateurs and pros. I came from the amateur ranks, so it was impossible for me to be his pal. He and a lot of the older pros at that time had something of a reverse snobbery ... they looked down on anybody who had been an amateur golfer.

STUDY ANNIKA'S STYLE

Annika Sorenstam could make a fine study for those from the men's tour who have problems getting the best out of themselves. She has a keen golfing brain that applies itself to careful planning of each round. She calls herself a "grinder", but if it is true, then so was Ben Hogan. For one thing, she never, ever tries to hit further than she can. Each shot is under firm control, and her judgment of distance is amazing. As for her putting, she is in the Kel Nagle class.

The Age, Melbourne, November 20, 1995

THE GAME'S ORIGINS

On my first visit to St Andrews I was told at the Rotary Club about a notion of the game's origin that appealed to me as eminently sensible. Of course, the story was told at St Andrews, but in deference to the claims of Holland that the Dutch invented golf, it happily fits them in, and I pass it on for what it's worth. No one can really contradict this, for the facts are lost in the mists of time. Golf arrived before anyone knew what it was.

In the 12th Century when Holland was the great trading nation and St Andrews was Scotland's Catholic ecclesiastical capital, there were small ships plying regularly across the North Sea, bringing goods from the Dutch and vice versa.

The town of St Andrews is and was set on a high bluff, rising up from the long beach at the far end of which the Firth of Tay bends in the estuary of the Eden River. Ships had to enter the river to anchor and unload, which left a haul of a mile and a bit from ship to town, across the soft dunes already turned to grass and whins in natural ecological evolution.

It was during these long walks to food and drink that the Dutch sailors took to hitting with sticks some sort of rolling ball or stone, counting as they went, perhaps to decide who would buy the drinks. Since the count must have reached a figure incalculable, it was easier to walk the course in stages, each stage marked and ended by "holing out" in some small depression in an area of general flatness and accessibility. These stages became six holes and we know them now, with holes on the high plateaus, except for the last that ended at the town steps.

The "course", it can be imagined, was anything but smoothly prepared. There would have been some close grassed areas clipped by the sheep, but it would have been mostly sand in the form of depressions scooped out by the animals making themselves shelter from the elements. The "players" would have had to play into and out of every kind of unsympathetic lie, and count each stroke.

The townsfolk fell for the charm of the game and took it up from the sailors, and thus started a craze that soon earned rebuke from the sovereign of the time, who wished subjects were better occupied with archery—far more useful in their own defence.

In time, the popularity of the play brought the problem of traffic jams, since those playing on the holes on the way out became entangled with the play coming in. The solution was to make two cups in each "green", spaced apart to avoid confusion. Thus was born the double green that is still with us today.

In fact, if one accepts that story of the origin, it is easy to see the Old Course in its present form as being directly evolved from the very birth of the game. There are today still six double greens with two holes and flags on each.

Golf Digest, July 1984

OLD COURSE EMOTIONS

There are plenty of golfers among the illustrious who do not like the Old Course at St Andrews. Discussion about St Andrews leads to an intensity of feeling such as no other course can. You either love it or hate it, at least on first acquaintance. Bobby Jones tore up his card at his first attempt at a score, and then later fell to its charms, ending up a confirmed aficionado.

Generally speaking though, one's opinion of the Old Course depends very largely on how you have dealt with it, or to put it another way, how the course has dealt with you.

My own experience has taught me the utmost respect for it as a championship test. No other course on the British Open rota quite measures up to it. It provides a difficulty second to none, combined with variation of wind from all directions. Temperature comes in all degrees, even during an Open week in the middle of high-summer July.

The course, almost entirely nature-made, has a subtlety no man can ever completely fathom. There is a razor edge between success and failure at every turn. It has two par threes, which makes the breaking of 70 a meritorious achievement. More than any other course I know on earth, the Old Course demands discipline and judgment—and both in abundance.

But St Andrews is not just a course. It is a Royal Borough with an ancient history, a ruined cathedral and castle, a modern university, five clubs and a passion for the game of golf unique. The whole town seems to give itself up to golf; the butcher, the baker and candlestick maker, their day's work done, can be seen scurrying down to the first tee to get their round in before dark.

If the Open champion comes to town, even as a tourist, a buzz goes around like a bush telegraph and before he knows it, hundreds of people are there to follow him off. At the end of the championship days, before the light finally fades near 11pm, you can see hundreds of St Andrews folk walking the course, pausing now and then where Nicklaus or Watson made a stroke earlier in the day, to swing the arms and hands in an imaginary execution of the memorable shot. Where else could it happen?

In modern times, when the course was formalised, the general territory became smoother, better kept. Bunkers were stabilised by revetting with turf sods, making walls almost vertical. This practice is seldom copied anywhere outside Britain. More is the pity. We would need fewer bunkers if each were more fearsome.

Golf Digest, July 1984

MAGIC UNDERFOOT

To describe the St Andrews course to those who have not yet felt its magic underfoot, it can be summed up as an adventure in risk-taking, and, on first tackle, an odyssey through a golfing minefield. There are 74 bunkers, most with names such as Scholar's, Cheape's Wig, Principal's Nose, Ginger Beer, Lion's Mouth, Nick's, Hell, Strath, Coffin and Mrs Kruger. Many are unnamed. But it makes eminent sense in the bars and cafes of the town to recite your misfortunes by reference to the particular point of disaster. "I got caught in Walkinshaw's" sounds better than "I got caught in that damned little trap to the right of the 13th fairway." Of course, there are no trees in sight except Cheape's Wood way off across the old rail line now extinct. Cheape, by the way, was the original adjoining landowner, who held grazing rights and the exclusive permit to take shells and grit from the links area. The early Cheape is immortalised as the bunker between the second and 17th, or to put it in St Andrewsese, between the Dyke and Road holes.

St Andrews never looks really easy from any angle, and truthfully it never is. It is a tough proposition for the best of professionals and a wholly terror for lesser mortals. Each of us in our golfing life goes about the training that gets us to the target in the most direct line, doing so by learning the "aiming of the stance". The last peek at the flagstick before the swing is always a habit. It is against our nature and instincts to hit away from the ultimate targets even though we know in our senses we have to do so to get close. It is this weakness, or lack of iron discipline, that gets us into trouble at St Andrews.

Looking out on the course, one sees a flat, open, rather dull expanse of territory rippled here and there, most noticeable as the sun sinks to the horizon. There is no sight, no hint of what lies ahead, except a clump of small bushes here and there off to the right side. To the experienced eye, there may be a clue indicating the line of a bunker beneath the surface, but little else. On most holes, just the top half or less of the flagstick is visible for the second shot. Distances are not easily measured with the eye. Nor is it apparent which line should be taken. Considering what lies between you and the flag, it is often not prudent to make a beeline for the objective, unless, of course, the shot will stop suddenly, which it will against the wind. But down hill or side, some strategy has to be worked out to get a close result. Herein lies the need for discipline of the sternest sort.

Golf Digest, July 1984

A RACING OF THE HEART

No-one who enjoys a game of golf could tee off at St Andrews on that first tee at the foot of the steps from the house without a racing of the heart. When I first looked out in September of 1954 it seemed like heaven. All my imaginings were proved true. There before me in the soft damp light of autumn lay this holy ground. So wide and keen was that first hole, sharing with the last the width of two cricket fields, and down at the end that dark surface ribbon that indicates the narrow burn (stream). And over it, banking it, the closer cut with the flag straight out in the wind.

Beyond in the near distance were the blackened railway sheds I would meet face to face come the 17th hole, and beyond that the Hills of Fife in the direction of Edinburgh. The railway sheds have gone, alas, but nothing else has changed. The North Sea rolls into the Firth of Tay along the beach to the right. The Royal Air Force Station at Leuchars sends up its jets from the distant pines, the seagulls the real landlords.

Golf Digest, July 1984

ST ANDREWS: THE HOLES

That first hole at St Andrews is classic simplicity. Called the Burn, it stretches away in full wide view for 374 yards (342 metres) between tee and flagstick. Nothing intrudes until the green edge, where lurks that "horrid sewer", the Swilcan, just four paces wide, flush with the putting green. The green itself is of enormous proportion, flat in the forecourt by the burn, but rising up into Himalayas at the rear, 30 yards (27 metres) on. In this age of target golf, the dimensions involved at this hole would seem to be ludicrous. The fairway virtually unmissable; the green a target like a football field; nothing it would seem to bring a moment's fear to a top player. Except the burn.

On championship days the flag in its cup is invariably near the burn. To get at it one must hit the green within a few yards of the water, otherwise the ball will bounce away to the back.

It is difficult for modern professionals to come to terms with the fact that on days when the wind is behind and the green is firm, it is just physically impossible to get anywhere near the flag with the approach shot. One has to be prepared to hit the second shot past the cup and to be content with that. Yet that inner weakness we all have will make us think again, somewhere near the start of the downswing, giving us a mental picture of the ball biting into the green just over the burn and miraculously braking right next to the flag. The next thing you know, you are in the burn.

It is this requirement of mental discipline to hit the shots away from the flags that makes the Old Course unique, so special and so searchingly fascinating. From the first hole through the last, it is a constant nagging temptation to attempt the impossible, to hit your approaches too near the gauntlet of straight-walled sand traps, to pull off shots that are commonplace elsewhere. If you don't discover and face this fact, you wall surely join the ranks of those who detest the place.

From the first hole, the course follows its way in a more or less steady direction northwest until the turn back east into the loop, beginning with the 8th. Considering the ever-present wind, it means a constant battle either to make distance with shots or apply your brakes to keep from going too far.

After the loop, the course reverses direction and relief or torture is your lot coming in. Going out with the wind behind and coming home against it, it is to my mind the easier task. The 2nd, 4th, 6th and 7th can be awfully long holes with a stiff wind into your teeth. Coming home it is somehow more manageable playing against it. It is not, of course, unusual to play out with the wind in one direction, say against, and then find out, at the turn, a change of tide and you're against it coming home as well.

Golf Digest, July 1984

THE ROAD HOLE

I would make a guess that among knowledgeable golfers, St Andrews' Road Hole, the 17th, is the world's most famous and infamous hole. Considering what has occurred there over the past century, it is a wonder the hole still stands in its original state. As a planner and builder of golf holes world-wide, I have no hesitation in allowing that if one built such a hole today you would be sued for incompetence and your effort would be destroyed. Yet to all those who have suffered at this demon, I offer a hand of friendship, for I have suffered, too, and to those who have passed its way without a mauling, I can only say, golfingly speaking, you haven't lived.

In almost every respect the Road Hole is unique. First the tee shot; nowhere else would you come across a tee shot that asks you to aim high across an out-of-bounds wall that blocks your view of the fairway you are trying to reach. A decade ago, the wall was a railway storage area. When the rail line was discontinued, the property went to a hotel development. The hotel has a high, bird-cage arrangement protecting the entrance, but the cage is effectively a substitute for the older wooden wall. There is an incentive to bite off all you can chew since the hole turns to the right and the nearer you can get to the OB line the better off you are, as I shall explain.

455 yards (416 metres) long, the 17th cannot be considered, in this age, a par 5 or three-shotter as it once was. Yet it is one hole where three shots might be more prudent than two.

The green is a tabletop of long, rectangular proportion, set "corner on" to the line of play. The table sides lift the green about a yard above the apron and into the left-hand side, about halfway along, is set a diabolical little bunker named Road Bunker. All around for yards and yards, the grass is cut close as a putting green, which encourages the use of the putter. The slope is cleverly varied just before the bunker, and one can only find a fairly large area short and left of the green, from which it is almost automatic that you putt into the bunker. At least the odds are stacked against you getting to the hole, which is always tucked behind the bunker. Here again, prudence should tell you to putt in another direction away from the flag, but that same old weakness that puts you into the burn at the first, will put you into Road Bunker at the 17th. But that is not the whole of it. To the right side of the tabletop green, and behind it, is a road of bitumen bordered by a strip of rough grass. Escape from the road is a matter of luck, because the side of the green is rough, uncut and abrupt. Victims usually take the putter from the road, or from across it, in an endeavour to get back up on the green, but the sharp slope will just as often reject your effort and send the ball back to you. And it's no use bashing it too hard either, because if it does jump too fast and hard, the ball will certainly race across the table off the other side—and often into the bunker.

Over the years, the road has decided many a match and championship. Recently, however, it has lost a little of its terror because the surface is smoother. But the road is still no place to go. And that has a big bearing on the second shot—that and the bunker.

The pot bunker is so named because of its shape—round, deep and sheer-sided, 12 feet (3.7 metres) in diameter. The Road pot is the best of its kind. A ball can nestle against the wall at any time. Count yourself lucky if your ball comes to rest where you can stand to play it forward toward the flag. More often it will nestle against the back wall, and the best you can do it play it backward. Tommy Nakajima took five strokes to get out of the Road Bunker in the 1978 Open, making television history before an audience of millions round the world. But he was not the first victim nor the last.

Going back to the second shot knowing now what is in front of you, it is wise, prudent and practical to lay up short with a club that will get you to the foot of the tabletop on the right front.

Then you have hurdled the last fence. It is plain sailing up the 18th, into the stadium of golf, onto that last green that Old Tom Morris had a hand in building, filling in a large crater but leaving just enough of it to create a Valley of Sin, which makes the front part of the putting green. (Doug Sanders three-putted that green in the 1970 Open and lost in a playoff the next day to Jack Nicklaus.)

When the Royal and Ancient Golf Club of St Andrews schedules its Open championship on the Old Course, it brings it "home". There was a time through the 1950s when a significant move was afoot to make the Old Course its permanent venue, in the same way that Augusta National annually hosts The Masters. Democracy had its way and the championship rotates through a list of superb and eminent clubs. None of them, however, has the status of seniority, eminence or authority of St Andrews Old. The R&A, in a way, lets the Open have its head to run about like a nervous hound, and then with a sharp pull on the leash, returns it to its kennel yard.

Golf Digest, July 1984

A RARE ACHIEVEMENT

I won my second British Open at St Andrews in 1955. I'd won on the course the previous September in the British Match Play, so I felt supremely confident going into the Open. My chief rival was Bobby Locke, who did win two years later on the Old Course (when I finished second), but I felt I could make lower scores on that course than anybody else and I went about my game that way. I tried to play sensibly, keep out of trouble, not three-putt ... no, I played in a very confident, high-expectation dream.

When I started my final round one shot ahead, and when I hit off, I knew exactly what I needed to score to win, as many challengers had finished their final round. I did, however, have a hiccup in the last round when I got caught in The Beardies—the bunkers on the par-five 14th fairway. The Beardies are horrible bunkers with straight walls. I drove into them, steering away from the out-of-bounds wall on the right and suffered the consequences—I had to play out backwards. I then hit a shot across Hell bunker, which was a daredevil thing to do in hindsight, but then I got caught in another bunker called The Grave, just near the green, and again I had to go backwards. I walked off with a seven and my lead had evaporated. But with some kind of luck, I birdied the next hole and I was back in the lead. That didn't exactly lock the door, but I got through the 16th, didn't try anything fancy at the Road Hole, playing it as a (bogey) five, which is what I got, and a four at the last was enough to win by two shots from Johnny Fallon, whom I'd played in the final of the Match Play.

Fallon was a Scot who had a club job at Huddersfield down in

Yorkshire. I have to say that, looking back, I do consider the win on the Old Course differently from the other four. Fifty years on, I'm glad I won at St Andrews. Very glad. It was, in hindsight, a rare achievement to win the Open on the Old Course and I feel lucky that I did it.

A VULNERABLE OLD COURSE

Anyone at St Andrews with a drink in his hand will tell you they have never seen the Old Course so green and lush. This is said not so much in praise, but trepidation. Everyone knows that the famous old layout is vulnerable in this day and age, such is the effect of modern equipment and professional skills. When the Old Course is soft, it may play a bit longer, but it certainly plays easier. The local population has observed this during the annual Dunhill matches in October. At that time, only the freezing temperatures offer much in the way of bite from the course. Even so, American Curtis Strange went around in 62 not many matches ago. Scores under 70 are relatively common. The course seems to lie helplessly disarmed.

This summer now, it is feared that a similar softness of the turf might even destroy the course's hallowed reputation as the supreme championship test. History tells us that the Old Course is at its fearsome best when it is parched dry, when the turf is scorched brown and dusty, and drives run 50 metres and more after hitting the ground. Then it is only a player's skill and prudence that keep him out of trouble in the form of the deep, straight-walled bunkers.

Approach work, too, is a matter of pitch and long run over hollow and ridge, a circumstance that modern professionals hate. Greens, too, in dry times can assume a glassy, cricket pitch-like appearance that makes putting a defensive exercise.

For the locals then, there is only dismay. There will be none of that this year. What they are hoping for then is a good wind just below hurricane strength to put Nick Faldo, Greg Norman, Nick Price and company to the fullest test, so that scores will be respectably high in the middle 70s, with par 72 a capital achievement. But would it matter if the winning score is a total of four 65s? So long as the best player won, I suppose it wouldn't. But then what would be said about the Old Course? Would it be judged to be inadequate for today's championship play? The answer might be "yes". Compared with Shinnecock Hills, used last month for the US Open, it might look like a pitch and putt. What the game of golf could do with now is a ball a few pennyweights lighter. One that would not pierce the wind so easily. One that would make par fives like par fives, as they used to be. A ball that would make the Old Course a tiger no matter what wind blew and however soft it was. However, I don't expect such dire results later this week. It may be windless for one day perhaps, but never for four. I would bet the winning score is respectable and that the best player wins, and the running of it will make fascinating viewing. The Old Course is not about to be mothballed yet.

The Age, Melbourne, July 19, 1995

NICE GUYS CAN WIN

There is something deeply warming about watching a modest battler take on high-profile stars and steal the pot. That is perhaps why golf is such a fine sport. Nice little guys sometimes win.

The Age, Melbourne, February 16, 1995

THE ROLE OF THE CADDIE

In my time, the best caddies would never speak unless spoken to. My feeling was that as long as he was punctual and sober, he knew the rules and was strong enough to carry the bag, he was fine by me.

Having caddies line up shots is pathetic, really. It shocks me. Anyone who needs such specific assistance is not a top player. He doesn't have my full applause because of the fact that he is always running for help for something. If he did it on his own, I would give him all the accolades because of his achievements.

Golf Digest, 1994.

THE PLACE FOR TROPHIES

I've never been one for showing off silver cups. You can't find any in any of my houses, except the ones that my wife, Mary, has put flowers in.

A WORLD BEATER

There is a tale told at Victoria Golf Club that legendary scratchmarker member Harry Williams once, on a Saturday, played the front nine in 29 strokes, whereupon he put his clubs in the locker and went off to the races. An embellishment tells that his playing partner put in his card for the bogey competition, recording nine losses for the back nine, and he consequently won the trophy. I have no doubt about the first part, but I discount the second. Such was the man's awesome reputation that apocrypha was bound to raise its head. As a young member of Victoria in 1947, I was invited to play with the fabulous man, but he turned up in his slippers, without clubs, and declined to play, so I never saw him hit a shot, although I have seen action shots of what looked like a magical swing—the length of John Daly's. Williams in his youth was hailed by Gene Sarazen as a world-beater, but in the 1930s the world was a far more distant place. Williams stayed at home and international fame eluded him.

The Age, Melbourne, November 12, 1994

DALY'S TOP NOTES

John Daly would be better off to leave his driving clubs in his locker, but when you're John Daly and the sponsors pay plenty and the people come to watch, well, you have to be John Daly, don't you? Otherwise there's no point. It would be like paying Pavarotti for a concert and he declined to sing the top notes. The world would complain.

The Age, Melbourne, March 2, 1995

A LONG SECOND SHOT

It is a pity that Ben Hogan's greatest feats came just before television, for a video of those times would be invaluable today. For Hogan was the first player in the world who devised a strategy to counter the modern architect. He took to driving short of the set trouble and risking a longer second shot. It paid off. He won five US Opens and one British (he could have won five of those, too, if he had tried). He thus set a tactical style of play that is with us today, if anyone takes it up. But it needs a special discipline and, I might add, a little courage to test your iron play from a long way further out. It seems a choice that no one wants. Modern players have a belief that if the driver is not working this week, then it will next time out, or the one after. It is a perfect recipe for inconsistency, and a good way to go broke if you play for prizes. It all seems so silly, because today's players are as accurate with five irons as they are with their sevens and eights. All that distance off the tee is hardly necessary.

The Age, Melbourne, November 11, 1994

VALE 'THE FOX'

When a fox appeared at Huntingdale the other day, I recognised Guy Wolstenholme's ghost. We held a memorial service for him at the course on another Masters occasion. Guy was known as Tally Ho, 'the Fox', by his Australian contemporaries, even before he won the first of his four Victorian Opens. The former Englishman was popular, and it seemed appropriate that the fox should pay us a visit on Thursday. Watching yesterday, I judged one had to play like a fox to dodge the multitude of dangers that loomed on a windy day with glassy-fast greens. Not many got through without losing a patch of fur.

The Age, Melbourne, February 19, 1994

MISGUIDED PUTTING ACTION

GARY Player, Arnold Palmer, Billy Casper, Kel Nagle, Bobby Locke and Isao Aoki all had one important thing in common. They never followed through on a putt less than two metres. The "stroke" they used was a natural use of wrists. The action was much more of a tap than a swing. The result was usually a positive strike towards the hole. I quote this piece of history because it is in marked contrast to the dozens of young budding Tour players I watch on the practice putting greens as we go from tournament to tournament. Almost to a man, the modern hopefuls practise a stiff-wristed, short-swung arm push towards a target, with an exaggerated follow-through. Where this particular technique originated, I am mystified.

I have been watching putting for more than 40 years and I have yet to see a successful putter who sets such an example. What I see is a rare and occasional "day out", when forearm strokers hole enough putts to convince themselves and others that this is the way to go. In between are always long bouts of failures, blamed on "misreading" or some other cause. Nobody, I note, questions the technique. The remedy for such failure is the locking of the wrists even tighter, so that the putting movement becomes even more mechanical and unnatural. This progression does not solve the problem either, but the sad result is that the victim is now farther down the road of no return. The next trick is the cross-handed grip and, after that, the grasping of the forearm with the free hand.

Beyond that is the abyss, the only refuge the broomstick. In the dimness of my memory is the well-meaning but, alas, misguided advice I received from supposedly knowledgeable people who told me I would never be a good putter because I had no follow-through. I wrestled with the recommended method most of my career and never got the hang of it. I would have been better advised to stick with what came naturally as a child. I might have joined Player, Palmer and co. The first step in the wrong direction is to accept that the putting stroke is different from every other shot. It is easy to adopt this belief because greens nowadays approach the purity of billiard tables. Since everything is in the player's favour, it is understood that the first putt can be (even should be) holed from anywhere. To miss from 10 metres is considered less than satisfactory. The assumption is that some mechanical style will achieve the results. And serious study of tournament play will find this is false, even nonsense. There are odds against any putt of any distance and the odds grow longer as the distance increases.

The only golfers who consistently lowered these odds were those I mentioned. Palmer, for example, in his hectic early years, was better than even money from two metres. Can anybody today among the arm-strokers claim such a rate?

The other obvious mechanical feature of Player, Palmer and co.'s putting was the long backswing. Even on short putts they drew the club back a long way. This I might suggest takes courage. They were all courageous, even outrageous players. There was, in their best times, not a moment of fear. The shortening of the backswing on putts becomes so evident on television as a player finds himself under pressure. It seems to be the first indication of stress, the first thing to alter as the tension mounts. It also leads to misses. I believe the mass of young tournament players is on the wrong putting track and that the further they travel down the wrong track, the more twisted and tangled becomes the whole performance on the green. The teaching is wrong, the whole theory is wrong. The results are disastrous. If the theory wasn't wrong, the whole entourage should be, by now, the best putters in history. The fact is that they might be, collectively, the worst. I do not see a Player or Nagle among them.

The Age, Melbourne, December 23, *1993*

LONG PUTTERS

I want the stroke banned, not the putter. I don't like the articulation of the wrist of the front arm. That's not a golf stroke. You can't tee off like that. Nor can you chip like that. The belly putter doesn't rile me, but it does take something away from the golfer to be seen doing it. It says: "I'm not very good, so I've had to come up with a trick."

I tried one when Orville Moody introduced one to the seniors tour. He was a wonderful player, but a poor putter. He went at it too fast and got himself into a terrible tangle. Some acquaintance of his introduced him to a long putter. I had a feel of it. Never played with it. It was so cumbersome. It's designed not to come off track, but it wasn't for me.

But I'm all for banning the articulation of the front arm.

One thing I like doing is using a rescue club to chip around the green. I don't think there's anything immoral about that. The golf clubs in the early centuries of golf, and photos of Old Tom Morris putting, show him not with a blade putter, but with a big-headed putter, like a driver. It's just about golf going back to where it was, and I have no problem with that.

HIT FOR THE CENTRE

Hitting for the centre of greens is uncommon these days. It is said to be throwing money away and no way to win. Doing the opposite is one certain way to miss cuts and throw tournaments away.

HEAT TAKES ITS TOLL

Eggs could be fried on the cart paths at the Vines yesterday, as players endured a trial by furnace on the first day of the Heineken Classic in Perth. Scores soared with the mercury. High-priced import, Welshman Ian Woosnam, took 44 strokes for his first nine, and finished on 80 only by the grace of some kindly bounces near the end. He spent a deal of time talking to the Xanthorrhoeas and Proteas, and once, at the 12th, he camped by the billabong, running up a six.

The Age, Melbourne, January 28, 1994

TOO MUCH PRAISE

When 100 per cent of a championship field is generous in its praise of the course, it should be concluded that something is wrong. At the Australian Open on Wednesday, Metropolitan received the seal of approval from the 150 who took practice rounds, which might have set off alarm bells. Championship courses are seldom universally popular.

The Age, Melbourne, 26 November, 1993

SOME LIKE IT HOT

Ray Floyd did not come through the Institute of Fine Swings. He came up through the School of Hard Knocks, which issues diplomas to those who survive the hot furnace of rough-and-tumble, gambling one's last dollar. At the school, there are no coaches, motivators or therapists. The course teaches self-reliance and hard concentration when your last chip is down. There is no one to turn to when you want a piece of coddling. There is always a shark circling and you had better not show fear and turn and run. Your only weapon is your courage, and experience teaches you how to use it. Such training makes a simple problem of a metre putt down a steep, sliding green, with millions of people watching you. Or with six holes to go, and a lead of one shot, it is nothing more to worry about than walking a tightrope. Life is like that—seldom wholly comfortable. Most players don't like the hot seat. A golfer with Floyd's qualifications and training runs a cool circulation system. The hotter it gets, the more he enjoys it.

The Age, Melbourne, November 25, 1993

SENIOR, THE QUIET MAN

I am an unabashed admirer of the golf playing of Peter Senior. I enjoy his uninhibited, full-swinging, attacking style. To me, no one else quite matches him in full flight—not even Greg Norman. I belong in a minority because Senior, despite his impressive list of winnings, goes largely unsung by Australia's sporting fans. He is not a person who craves publicity. I wonder what he would do with it, as he seems perfectly content without it. When he does start in an event ... he has absolutely nothing to lose. Other famous achievers—and yet-to-be-achievers—have no such freedom. It must be awful to be Greg Norman, expected to win every time out.

The Age, Melbourne, February 19, 1993

IMITATING GREATNESS

Greg Norman was not himself yesterday. He was Jack Nicklaus. As a result of spending five days at Port Douglas last week, playing skins games with his idol, it is now easy to mistake our man for a younger version of the greatest winner of championships the game has known. On every shot yesterday, it was apparent that Norman has adopted the mannerisms of his role model, at least to the point of addressing the ball. First, he would take a position four paces behind the ball, club in his right hand, left arm free to shake loose his shirt. Then he would step into his stance with the same measured stride that has marked the Nicklaus method for nigh on

30 years. Even his waggles are Nicklausian, and the shifting of his weight between heel and toe is a clear imitation of the older man. In total, it was an "old look" Norman and a better one at that. It set a revised standard of balance and a slower, more effective rhythm. Norman seemed like a star reborn yesterday. He is not the first one to fall under the spell of a senior, dominant personality. We have all done it in our time and, if it means the rejuvenation of a technique off the rails, it is an excellent thing.

The Age, Melbourne, February 17, 1989

SNEAD, A VERY HUMAN GOLFER

Sam Snead was a unique talent. He died late last week aged 89. That would have been the highest number he ever made in his long career. He first came to Australia in 1959, as one of a pair for the US Canada Cup team at Royal Melbourne. Then he and I played a one-off exhibition at Yarra Yarra at 4.30 on an autumn afternoon in 1973, when 7000 people turned out to watch him.

Snead was one of a legendary triumvirate. The other two, Ben Hogan and Byron Nelson, made up a pantheon of golfing gods. Hogan and Nelson set records for the books. Snead, on the other hand, made an indelible impression on countless people's minds as the most gifted natural golfing athlete that ever lived. He won, it is calculated, more than 120 serious tournaments which included a British Open and four Masters, but, inexplicably, no US Open. He was unique in his longevity. Because of his gift, he played at the highest level of professional golf even into his 70s. He came to the

2000 British Open at St Andrews at the age of 87 (54 years after his first and only visit when he won), to participate in the four-hole parade of former champions on the eve of the main event, showing still his beautifully rhythmic swing and immaculate timing over the home holes.

At his peak through the '40s and '50s, Snead was acknowledged as the world's longest driver. Yet Snead seldom "let loose". He came to the top in an era of control where one hit one's tee shots with care. He was never captured on film in the trees playing miraculous recovery shots. His second shots were invariably played from the fairway—and from the centre of it as well. If he had a weakness, it was his play on the greens. His putting was often pathetic, as he missed time and again from short distances for birdies, which seemed to destroy his exuberance, until he resorted to straddle putting (which was soon outlawed), ending up trying to hole putts "side saddle". Yet everyone sympathised and forgave him.

I watched him play an awesome 18-hole playoff for the 1954 US Masters against Hogan, which he won with a 70 to Hogan's 71. It was the most fascinating golfing spectacle I ever witnessed. His effervescent humour was mostly homespun, as one would expect from a man from the West Virginia mountains, and his early travels prompted some famously naïve responses.

His "manager", Fred Corcoran, told of the day of his first Los Angeles Open when Corcoran produced a copy of *The New York Times* with Sam's photograph on the sports pages. The 20-year-old tyro expressed his surprise and some indignation: "How'd they get my picture? I ain't never been to New York."

At a Masters dinner in the early '50s, he was asked if there was anything in golf that he was afraid of, to which he replied: "Yes, a three-foot putt downhill—and Ben Hogan." Snead could be blunt to foolish questions, too. To an innocent who opined: "Gee it must be really tough to play the (US) tour", Snead, with scarcely a glance, replied: "Yep, sure is" and after a pregnant pause came, "if you can't play." It just about summed it all up.

For Sam Snead, playing professional golf was like a walk in the park, and he loved nothing better. It was the adulation of the crowds, particularly the feminine ones, and the camaraderie of the locker room. He was never a smoker nor a drinker, until his later years when I caught him having a little brandy nip before tee off. "Just to settle the nerves," he said. He was a very human golfer.

The Age, Melbourne, May 29, 2002

SIR ROBERT MENZIES

Sir Robert Menzies was a very friendly person. Our paths crossed when he came to watch the 1959 Canada Cup at Royal Melbourne. Prime Ministers from that time liked to be seen at sporting events, however I do think he had a genuine interest in watching sport, including golf, although I don't think he ever played.

I used to spend a month in the Windsor Hotel (in Melbourne) at the end of the season. I'd come back from the American tour and it was a very reasonable thing to stay at The Windsor, and suit 2A on the first floor was R. G. Menzies'.

Late afternoon I'd get a knock on the door from Hughie Dash, who was his press secretary, and he'd say: "The boss wants to see you for a drink." I'd go up, have a beer while he'd have something and we'd have a chat. I suppose I became something of a confidant.

Later, when Sir Robert was confined to a wheelchair, I'd sit with him at Carlton games.

THE HUNGRY SPORTS MACHINE

Golfers, in a previous age, relied on their wits rather than modern technology. I am grateful I was born when there were no electronics to confuse life. Radio was enough to satisfy my curiosity. The rest of my amusements came out of my own head. Life was a sort of general bliss. When it came to playing sport, I held a growing image of myself, batting like Don Bradman, playing tennis like John Bromwich, kicking a football like Fred Hughson, and playing golf like Sam Snead. Of course, I had never set eyes on Sam Snead. I just imagined in what manner he played.

How I actually looked to others was of no possible concern. What occupied my entire waking moments was how to get from A to B in the fewest possible strokes. By trial, and plenty of error, I refined this down to an effective procedure (I avoid the word "technique"). More often than not, I achieved my hopes. Once there, proven under fire, the system was cotton-woolled and sealed in watertight security. I made sure that no one intruded on my private territory. I was fearful of destruction of my precious knowledge.

Thus it is that I cry for the fate of so many talented young sportsmen and women who are born into the world of "scientific" intrusion into their personal lives, coupled with the horrible truth that sport has become a passport to wealth—if one is prepared to surrender to the charms of media spotlighting. The wealth flows sideways and in some cases upwards, to agents, so-called managers, motivators, image-makers and, at the end of the chain, the coaches. It must appear to a young sportsperson just entering the arena, that these adjuncts to themselves are essential baggage, and that it is impossible to achieve one's goals if you take on the world on your own. The first consequence of this surrender is to lose one's self-reliance. It is, of course, not in the interests of all those who tag along, to have their "person" making their own decisions. Out in the loneliness of the arena, though, the strongest, most self-reliant come out on top.

Now, apart from the "minders", we have the advent of the computer. A golfer can carry a laptop, which goes in tandem with a camera, which can video his swing; it's then sent by e-mail to his swing adviser, who will immediately spot any "bugs" and respond immediately. I have a feeling of horror. For a start, having yourself depicted in action, for your own inspection and gratification, is a dangerous narcissistic practice, which can utterly destroy an ego. It is a multiple demolition to discover your own ugliness. Furthermore, it is a doubtful system of looking at yourself from outside in, instead of looking from inside out (I believe that the crash of Ian Baker-Finch had much to do with his concentration on what he looked like, instead of what he thought like).

The self-confidence and ego that all winning sportspeople have is such a delicate mechanism that it cannot be dependent on another person. It has to be nurtured from within, protected by one's own defences and against unwarranted intrusions of mental viruses. Golf has a bigger mental component than almost all other games, especially ball games. Its big champions all mastered the mental aspect. All had total self-confidence. Some were super-egoists. None depended on others in times of stress. None gazed at themselves on the screen. I have no favourite among the many youngsters I come across. I wish them all well. I will get a huge warmth out of seeing them prosper.

What I observe, though, is a wasteland of destruction of young talent. The giant professional sport machine devours them for breakfast and spits out the pips, while preparing a new meal to feed its voracious appetite. What we need is a Salvation Army of sport, to pick up the detritus and discards, to put them back on the track, freed from the dependence of management and manipulation.

The Age, Melbourne, October 27, 1998

AN AMATEUR GREAT

Few, if any, champion amateur golfers, now or in the future, will stay within the confines of amateur status long enough to enter the record book. The rewards of crossing the line into professional ranks are too enticing to forgo. It wasn't always so. Doug Bachli died on Wednesday after a long illness that kept him away from the golf course for almost a decade, yet his record of exploits will mark him as one of the foremost amateurs of his time worldwide. For it was in Scotland in 1954 that he won the British amateur championship, beating American giant Bill Campbell in a memorable final at Muirfield.

His visit to Britain included a place in the Australian amateur team of four that took out the Eisenhower Cup trophy, played in its inaugural year at St Andrews. Bachli starred in that squad, which included Peter Toogood from Tasmania, Bob Stevens from South Australia and Peter Heard from New South Wales. The trophy was then presented by the illustrious Bobby Jones. The winning of it boosted Australia's golfing image immeasurably.

Bachli was a Victoria Golf Club member from 1946. He came from Canberra as a scratch golfer (and a champion swimmer), slotting into a pennant team that reigned supreme through the '40s. Working for his publican father, he had plenty of time for golf, which enabled him to compete in amateur championships around Australia. Bachli won two Australian amateur titles and 13 club championships at Victoria. His strength as a player came from a stocky build, on which he based an orthodox swing with a tidy rhythm. As he showed during his great match with Campbell at Muirfield, his driving was infallible and he capped this off with a real flare for holing out. Had he come along 20 years later, he would have undoubtedly tried his hand at playing for prizes, but we can only speculate where that would have led. Those of us who played with him will recall his endless humour and his great passion for the game. He was one of the last real amateur golf champions who brought lustre to the sport and his country as well.

The Age, Melbourne, January 7, 2000

WIND PLAY

To play in the wind, you must maintain a full swing with a full cock of the wrists ... horizontal at the top of the swing and beyond if you can. People who shorten their swing in order to keep some sort of control fall by the wayside. It was pathetic to watch Tiger Woods in 1998, the year Mark O'Meara won at Royal Birkdale. Woods finished third, but his efforts in trying to keep the ball low were quite comical to watch. He shortened his swing by not cocking his wrists fully so he couldn't actually crush the ball into the turf and send it off on a low trajectory. John Daly, on the other hand, is a master of wind play because he has such a long swing. He keeps the ball quail-high by keeping a long swing, delaying the uncoiling of the wrists so that the club has less loft than normal. By hitting it hard at the same time, he can drill a two-iron about 200 metres at just two or three metres high. But you cannot play shots low into the wind with a shortened, abbreviated swing. The secret is a steady nerve at the top of the swing ... not worrying about rushing back to get to the ball.

USING LOFT

If you're going to run the ball along the ground, you don't want to only half run it along the ground. Don't send it in the air for half its journey. That's hard to judge. Start it with just enough loft to get it running. Like a four-iron or, if you can, a putter. A four-iron will give you a bit of backspin, but a putter won't. If you're going to wedge it up, take the most loft you've got. Not in between.

A GLOVE DOESN'T MATTER

There's no right or wrong to wearing a glove. When I played in the '50s and early '60s, there was no such thing as a golf glove. A few people had half a glove ... a kind of mitt. The great players like Ben Hogan and Byron Nelson didn't use gloves and, being a young emulator, I thought that if it was good enough for them to play bare-handed, then it was good enough for me. I think if I'd come through the '70s and '80s, I would have used a glove like everybody else. I don't use one now, but to be honest, on hot days when you get sweaty, and on cold days without any feel in your fingers, it's a big advantage to wear a tight-fitting leather glove. My general observation, however, is that it doesn't matter. Some take it off to putt, some even to chip, but this would only be to strengthen their confidence.

STANDING OUT

Today's golfers seem to have accepted a uniform: short-sleeve shirt with some kind of logo, a painter's cap, common shoes made by the leading manufacturers, and dark glasses. If I was setting out to make a career from golf, I would wear different clothes. Greg Norman tried to be different with his hat, with his long blond hair coming from underneath. He stood out and I'm sure that was to his advantage. It helps with marketing, but it's also intimidating in its way. If you wear something distinctive, then obviously you are full of confidence and want to be yourself. I used to like to wear greys with white shoes and I played a lot in cardigans with a button-up front which made me look unlike other people ... long or short-sleeve, depending on the weather. I liked that look. Nobody uses it now. Perhaps it's time to bring it back. Golfers today look the same and they all swing alike. You don't see anybody swinging like a Lee Trevino or Doug Sanders. They all look alike and it's a problem for the overall image of golf playing.

NO MAGIC ON TELEVISION

Golf's biggest problem is trying to find a way to make it more thrilling. It is one man against a whole field, so it doesn't have any element of spite. There are no physical collisions like football. But it is a game that can be fully appreciated on television. I have watched very closely its development on television since the commercial networks brought their way into it. Now, there are only 40 minutes of actual golf every hour. The other 20 minutes are taken up by advertising.

Golf's problem is that there are no natural breaks. When golf goes to an ad, there's actually a lot happening. Shots will be taped so that when they return from their three minutes of ads, the director runs the tape. You're not seeing 'live' golf. In cricket, there's a natural break at the end of each over, in football after every goal. Ads, therefore, can be tolerated during natural breaks. It's not tolerated in golf because the viewer knows the competition is continuing. There's also a problem with the repetition of the ads, and that detracts from the whole production and reinforces irritation. This affects ratings and, if the commercial television networks dump golf, there's no future at all for tournaments. So it's serious. I watch the US television coverage and it's in a similar plight. They don't get enough variety into their golf; there's little variation in the weather, players look alike, even the courses look alike. It has lost its magic.

GOLFING, USA

My first visit to the States was really a culture shock. First, everything cost about twice what it cost in Australia. The golf was strange because the courses were usually wet and not cut very close. The tour itself played on a lot of really poor, second-class courses.

On the positive side, there were many things I enjoyed immensely. I enjoyed the comfort of the hotel accommodations, and the food, like the magnificent steaks we all ate. And of course, the luxury cars. There wouldn't have been one Cadillac in Australia at that time. Also the tremendous warmth and friendliness of people I found everywhere.

Golf Digest, 1994

WHERE ARE THE CHARACTERS?

In the summer of 1950, I decided to spend time playing in the United States. Their first event of the year was the Bing Crosby tournament on the great courses of Pebble Beach, Cyprus Point and Monterey Peninsula. I set off in a propeller-driven plane from Melbourne that took about 35 hours to get to California. I was met by a Dunlop representative in San Francisco and driven down to Monterey. I went to sleep in a little bed-and-breakfast place and was so jet-lagged that I almost slept through my tee-off time. Jim Ferrier left a set of clubs for me, a new set of Wilsons, but they didn't suit me. So I was battling with a new set of sticks in strange surroundings and struggling to stay awake, so I didn't do very well.

The following week was the Los Angeles Open at a terrible public links course in that sprawling city and I was shocked by the standard of the course. The following week I was in Tuscon, Arizona, and by that time I'd had enough. I'd played with Cary Middlecoff, Sam Snead, Jimmy Demaret ... it was a valuable insight and I knew what I had to aspire to to be a top golfer. I didn't actually run out of money, but I got pretty low and went home. But I made some friends and when I went back again the next year they were very nice to me. I'd been taken under the wing of the Demaret gang. Jimmy was a jovial fellow and one of the very best players. He had a way of making friends ... of making everyone feel comfortable. He had a group of golfing friends, including Jack Burke, Lew Worsham, who'd won a US Open, and Clayton Hefner, who was also a great card player and one of the few people to turn down an invitation to play at Augusta.

The greens at Augusta used to do outrageous things in those days. Bobby Locke told them to keep their invitation, too. There was a time one day when Hefner rushed to the first tee from a card game in which he was winning. He used to tee the ball up very high and, in his haste, the club went right under the ball. It popped up very high but not very far … 20 or 30 metres off the tee. He told the caddie to leave the ball where it was and he went back to the card game. You don't get many characters like that. "Terrible" Tommy Bolt was another. We recently saw a young American, Ricky Barnes, get fined for a temper-tantrum at the Masters at Huntingdale. I think a warning would have sufficed. We need player reactions … spontaneous, natural reactions. There's no point in every player being perfectly behaved.

THE FLEMING CONNECTION

Ian Fleming was a keen player in the pro-am tournaments that popped up around the London area in the mid 1950s. I remember him writing a very amusing piece in The Sunday Times about one of these events entitled "Nightmare Among The Mighty", which was about partnering me, as the Open champion. I found him a very friendly and delightful man and my wife and I subsequently spent time with him socially. He may have been the creator of James Bond, but on the golf course, he was subject to the same weaknesses as the rest of us. A delightful man.

PLAYING IN THE CANADA CUP

The Canada Cup was inspired by a passionate golfer, and visionary, but not a Canadian! Its founder was John J. Hopkins, president of the US multi-national company General Dynamics, a company he originally formed, and chairman of its subsidiary Canadair. From this link was born the Canada Cup. The first Cup was played in Montreal in 1953. Ossie Pickworth and I were invited to represent Australia. It was a very low-key affair in its early days, with only seven nations competing for the inaugural trophy. It has now grown to be the World Cup, with the winning team receiving the John Jay Hopkins Cup. Kel Nagle and I teamed up for the first time in 1954 and we won. The Argentines had been leading, but they made a hash of the last final round while Kel and I had a pretty smart last nine holes.

In 1959, the event was brought to Melbourne. It had an expanded sponsorship ... Hopkins had died. In '55, when it was played in Washington, it was revealed he had an advanced cancer. The sponsorship was taken up by a group of American companies and it was decided to take it around the world. It was played at Royal Melbourne (for the first time the composite course was used in a championship) and Kel and I were nominated to be the Australian team, probably by virtue of what we'd won. It was a great career highlight for both of us. The crowds were big, by our standards, the then Prime Minister, Robert Menzies was there and the course was an enormous hit with the American writers. Kel and I won and I think that event really helped put Australian golf on the global scene, and we've been there ever since.

NAGLE'S MAGIC

In 1960, Kel Nagle and I were invited to defend our Canada Cup title in Ireland and we were presented with first-class tickets that we could use months before the event. I was in the US and Kel came along in May and joined me. In a week when there was a gap in the program, I said: "Come on, we'll go to the MacGregor warehouse, in Dallas, and see what new clubs we can buy." We opened a few boxes ... drivers, three and four-woods. And, of course, we had to pay. Kel picked out a beautiful set of woods and he immediately began to play better.

The first week that he had those clubs, Kel was pipped by one shot for the Fort Worth invitational tournament by Julius Boros. Kel hadn't been playing well until then ... in all honesty he played something of a supporting role when we won the Canada Cup at Royal Melbourne ... but suddenly he loomed like a real winner. A couple of weeks later, I suggested he get rid of his irons, which had been made in Sydney and were really pretty weak. But Kel was intensely loyal and he said: "Oh no, they pay me to use these." I asked him what they were paying him and, after he told me, I said: "Kel, you can win that in one day. Don't tie yourself down to something that's not the best you can get." We had a practice round soon after with Bobby McAllister, an acquaintance of ours, and Bobby was trying out a new set of Spalding irons. He told me they didn't suit him so I asked if I could loan them to Kel. Kel had a hit with them and it transformed him. He was suddenly a top player. We then had to convince Spalding to give Kel the clubs. It took a bit of convincing. They hadn't heard of Kel Nagle and didn't think he could win anything, but I spoke to the fellow and said: "You'll be sorry if you let him slip out of your hands. Give him the clubs and let him play with them."

A week or two later, we went to Ireland to play the Canada Cup. Kel played well and finished fourth and the next week was at the British Open at St Andrews. Armed with his new equipment and his new-found confidence, and still with his magic putting, and with me showing him how to keep out of the St Andrews bunkers and play second shots away from the flags sometimes, Kel won the Centenary Open. It was a shock to him and a shock to everybody else, but in my view, I nominated him. I finished ninth, four or five shots back. I couldn't putt like Kel. He was magic. When he finished, he had no way of making it through the crowd to his hotel, but needed a jacket for the presentation. I'd finished some time earlier and so I took off my jacket and gave it to him. In the picture taken of him, holding the trophy, he is wearing my jacket.

A HAPPY ATTITUDE HELPS

I passed on to my Presidents Cup team that a happy attitude helped you play well. So I always had a smile on my face, or thought I did. Peter Alliss used to remark that I was unusual in this regard. He reckoned I was enjoying myself and not trying hard enough but it was quite wrong to make this assumption. I was trying my hardest, but I was enjoying it. I simply played my best when I was in a happy mood. You too can self-generate happiness by saying: "Here I am, playing golf and it's better than working."

A PRIZE-WINNING JACKET

It's always advisable to attend the last round of a tournament with a jacket. At the 1956 Open, which I won, at Royal Liverpool, or Hoylake, as it is called, I couldn't get back to the hotel to get my jacket. It was customary in those days to get dressed up to accept the first prize. A friend of mine, a captain from Royal Melbourne, Max Shaw, had a beautiful cashmere, grey jacket. I asked if I could borrow it. It was about the right size. Over I went to get the prize. I thanked Max for his jacket and handed it back and, months later, he sent his jacket to the dry-cleaners in Melbourne and found a cheque for £1200 in the pocket. It was the first prize cheque and I'd forgotten to get it out of the pocket.

LOVING THE CAPTAINCY

I regard captaining the Presidents Cup as one of the most useful things I have done in my golfing life. It was a marvellous experience. It's far more satisfying than individual golf and that's why there's such an aura around the Ryder Cup. The captain's role is, simply, to keep his players happy and thereby get the best out of them.

In Melbourne in 1998, I didn't have to do much. They were all keyed up and full of joy. With more or less the same team two years later in Washington, they played like a lot of hairy goats. They couldn't pull themselves together, which was a shock.

Shigeki Maruyama, the first day I saw him play in Washington, had shortened his swing and couldn't hit his hat, so I asked the interpreter why he swung so short and why didn't he swing like he did at Royal Melbourne—a long, flowing swing. The interpreter replied: "He's doing weightlifting and, with his muscles, he can't do it." I suggested he get out of the gym and get back to where he was. He typified the whole team. The American team was also far more powerful than the ragged team they had in Melbourne. I don't know whether the hot weather in Melbourne didn't suit them or the early-morning hit-offs or the coffee, but they were not at their best.

People expressed some surprise when I partnered Frank Nobilo with Greg Turner in Melbourne. I have respect for Nobilo and I felt I could get him going. I could see why he was struggling. And Turner's a winner. I thought, as two Kiwis, they'd make a good combination, but then I learned that they didn't get on together. For the sake of the match, they decided to bury the hatchet and became very valuable.

At the reception to my marriage to Mary in 1960 at the Park Lane Hotel in London—the happiest day of my life.

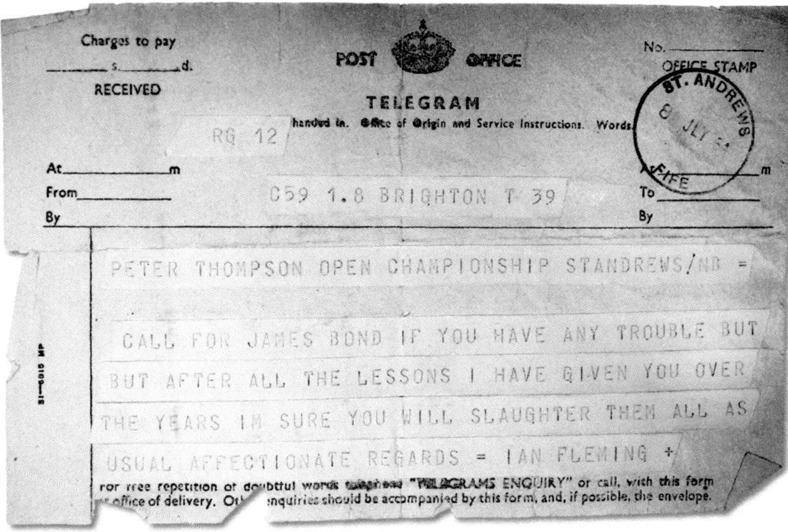

Charges to pay
s. d.
RECEIVED

POST OFFICE
TELEGRAM

No.
OFFICE STAMP
ST. ANDREWS
8 JLY 64
FIFE

RG 12 handed in. Office of Origin and Service Instructions. Words.

At m
From
By

C59 1.8 BRIGHTON T 39

To
By

PETER THOMPSON OPEN CHAMPIONSHIP STANDREWS/NB =

CALL FOR JAMES BOND IF YOU HAVE ANY TROUBLE BUT
BUT AFTER ALL THE LESSONS I HAVE GIVEN YOU OVER
THE YEARS IM SURE YOU WILL SLAUGHTER THEM ALL AS
USUAL AFFECTIONATE REGARDS = IAN FLEMING +

For free repetition of doubtful words telephone "TELEGRAMS ENQUIRY" or call, with this form at office of delivery. Other enquiries should be accompanied by this form, and, if possible, the envelope.

HERALD & WEEKLY TIMES

Top: A telegram from Ian Fleming, the creator of James Bond, wishing me luck in the 1964 British Open. Fleming was a keen player in pro-am tournaments. My wife and I spent time with him socially.

Bottom: Another airport farewell. I'm holding Fiona's hand and then, from left, Peta-Ann, Mary and Andrew. Professional golf is tough on young families.

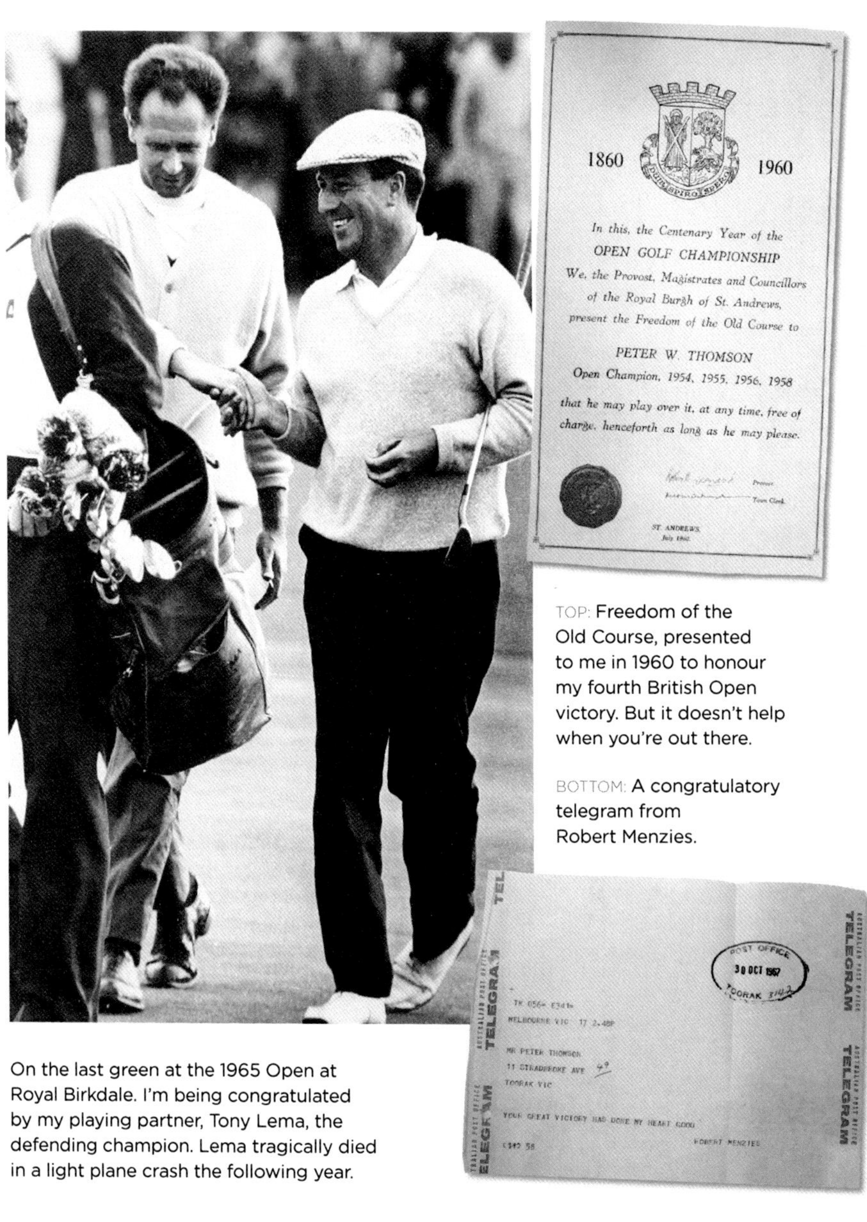

1860 1960

In this, the Centenary Year of the
OPEN GOLF CHAMPIONSHIP
We, the Provost, Magistrates and Councillors of the Royal Burgh of St. Andrews, present the Freedom of the Old Course to

PETER W. THOMSON
Open Champion, 1954, 1955, 1956, 1958

that he may play over it, at any time, free of charge, henceforth as long as he may please.

Provost
Town Clerk

ST. ANDREWS

TELEGRAM

POST OFFICE
30 OCT 1967
TOORAK 3142

TK 056 E341
MELBOURNE VIC 17 2.48P

MR PETER THOMSON
11 STRADBROKE AVE 49
TOORAK VIC

YOUR GREAT VICTORY HAD DONE MY HEART GOOD

ROBERT MENZIES

TOP: Freedom of the Old Course, presented to me in 1960 to honour my fourth British Open victory. But it doesn't help when you're out there.

BOTTOM: A congratulatory telegram from Robert Menzies.

On the last green at the 1965 Open at Royal Birkdale. I'm being congratulated by my playing partner, Tony Lema, the defending champion. Lema tragically died in a light plane crash the following year.

With daughter Peta-Ann after winning my first Australian PGA title at Metropolitan GC, in 1967.

GETTY IMAGES

On the podium with my son, Andrew, after winning the 1967 Australian Open at Commonwealth in Melbourne.

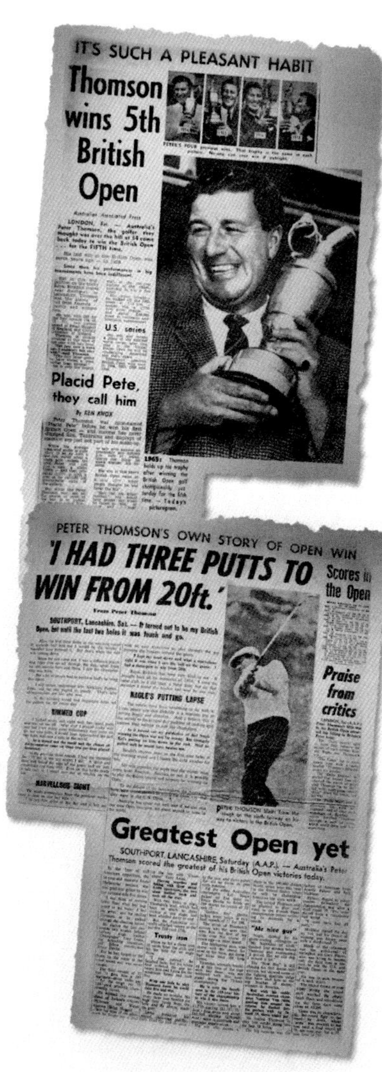

IT'S SUCH A PLEASANT HABIT

Thomson wins 5th British Open

Australian Associated Press

LONDON, Sat. — Australia's Peter Thomson, the golfer they thought was over the hill at 34 came back today to win the British Open — for the FIFTH time.

U.S. series

Placid Pete, they call him

By KEN KNOX

1965: Thomson holds up his trophy after winning the British Open golf championship ... for the fifth time. — Today's picturegram.

PETER THOMSON'S OWN STORY OF OPEN WIN

'I HAD THREE PUTTS TO WIN FROM 20ft.'

From Peter Thomson

SOUTHPORT, Lancashire, Sat. — It turned out to be my British Open, but until the last two holes it was touch and go.

RIMMED CUP

NAGLE'S PUTTING LAPSE

MARVELLOUS SIGHT

Scores in the Open

Praise from critics

PETER THOMSON ... on the sixth fairway on his way to victory in the British Open.

Greatest Open yet

SOUTHPORT, LANCASHIRE, Saturday (A.A.P.). — Australia's Peter Thomson scored the greatest of his British Open victories today.

Trusty iron

"Mr nice guy"

TOP: Another article about my 1965 win. Mind you, I also lost 25 British Opens.

BOTTOM: A newspaper article saluting my fifth British Open win in 1965. "Greatest Open yet"... that may be a slight overstatement.

Giving guidance to a grown-up Peta-Ann. She's known as 'Pan' because her siblings always struggled with the double Christian name.

TOP: With my daughter, Pan, and my wife, Mary, after my first win on the Seniors Tour in Palm Springs, California, in September 1984. After I won, Pan told the media I would win 10 more times that year. I won nine. My tenth came a month after that year had ended—in October 1985.

GETTY IMAGES

At the opening ceremony of the Presidents Cup in 2000 at the Robert Trent Jones golf club in Gainsville, Virginia. We were quite soundly thrashed. I'm with the very astute American captain, Ken Venturi, the 1964 US Open champion, and President Bill Clinton.

A line-up of Open champions on the first tee at St Andrews in 1978. Back row (left to right): Roberto de Vicenzo, myself, Bob Charles, Johnny Miller, Tom Weiskopf, Jack Nicklaus, Bobby Locke. Front row (left to right): Max Faulkner, Fred Daly, Tony Jacklin, Henry Cotton, Arnold Palmer, W.M. Muirhead (Capt. R. & A.), Tom Watson, Gary Player, Kel Nagle.

HERALD & WEEKLY TIMES

A happy moment with Mary. The occasion was during the Presidents Cup at Royal Melbourne in 1998.

KIMBAL BAKER

A photograph of me taken in 2003 at Royal Birkdale to commemorate the 50th anniversary of my first British Open win.

When this book was first published, in 2005, Peter Thomson wrote this caption to this photo: "I've got to this ripe old age in good health without too many enemies. That's all one can ask." He died in June, 2018, aged 88. That personal reflection remained true to the end, although his health had deteriorated in the last few years of his life—Steve Perkin.

I was very sad and reluctant to leave out Robert Allenby, but he'd gone off his game and there was no indication he was getting hold of it again. You see these things and you get to know the players and their personalities. It's interesting to listen to their hopes and wishes and their secret fears... "Ooo, I'd rather not play him if you don't mind." And sometimes I felt that, if I was in his place, I wouldn't like to play that fellow, either. But it has to be.

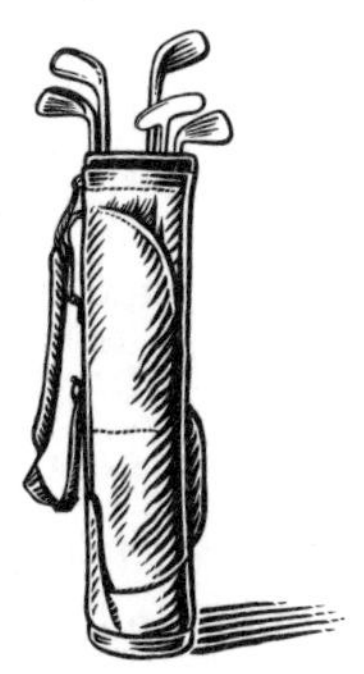

SUCCESS IN BRITAIN

I had most of my golfing success in Britain, I think because the kind of golf required suited me nicely. It's weather golf, and when it wasn't weather golf, it was hard ground, and that's right up my street. People I couldn't beat in other circumstances I could beat easily on a hard, bouncy course. It's not easy to make low scores on a hard, bouncy course because the ball can bounce out of control. It requires judgement. I learned early that Royal Park in Melbourne was like concrete in summer, so I always wondered what the ball was going to do once it hit the ground. Today, the players all know—the ball's going to spin back to you.

You couldn't putt from off the green as I found you could later (in Scotland) because it wasn't smooth enough. To end up on the green, you had to drop the ball short of the green through the air and let it bounce forward. That's how I learned to judge the bounce of the ball and, from the ages of 20 to 40, I was very good at it. I knew how to handle hard ground while most of the people I played against didn't.

In the year this book was first published (2005) I'm to be made an honorary member at Walton Heath in Surrey. I won three match play championships there, all of them in the summer when the ground was as hard as concrete. Some holes there are almost downhill. You've got to drop the ball 60 metres short of the green and let it run on. Not one club in Sydney, his home town, has made Kel Nagle an honorary life member. Stupid, isn't it?

THINK ABOUT THE BOUNCE

Golf is a game played by the bounce of the ball. Playing in Britain in summer, the ground gets like concrete, and a shot of 200 metres is actually a shot of 180 metres carry and then a good 20 metres of run. Unless you plan it that way, you won't find the target. Thinking about what will happen to the ball on the ground is just as important as what will happen to it through the air.

WINNING THE FIRST HOLE

When playing match play, I always liked to win the first hole. It set me up ... let me think I was on my way. If I lost it, it just added to the work I had to do. In the origins of golf, people didn't keep score except in holes won and lost. They played match play for the first 100 years.

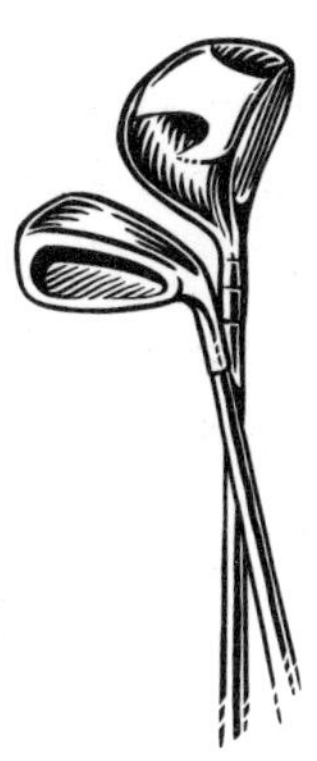

THE FIGHT IN THE DOG

I've always felt that, if the golf circuit was match play—knock-out, as tennis is—that there would be fewer winners. The stronger personality invariably wins match play matches. It's a dog-fight and the dominant dog will always win.

TENDON TRAUMA

It was about 1975. I was in Bangkok, staying in a hotel. I jumped out of bed one morning. The air-conditioning had been on, I was cold and my tendons were tight. I had to race to the course to make my tee-off time and my first hit for the day was my opening drive. I heard a tendon in my left wrist snap—it went off like a rubber band. I went down to the green to play my pitch, but when I got to the top of the swing and cocked my wrists, I knew I'd torn it. I had to pull out right then and there. I was advised to rest for three weeks, which I did, then I gave it a try. I strapped it up and went out to play, but I did more damage to it. Through the late '70s and early '80s, when I played the seniors in America, I was petty careful of it. I couldn't over-work it. In the locker room, they used to always have a barrel filled with drinks and ice. Before I'd play, I'd stick my hand in it up to my wrist and hang on until I was aching with cold, then I'd go over to the tap and turn the hot tap on. That's how I'd treat it. Truthfully, it's never been any good since.

LEARNING TO COMMENTATE

My first golf commentating was with the BBC in the 1970s with Henry Longhurst at Royal Birkdale for a Ryder Cup match. It was very interesting working with Longhurst and we had a director who drilled into us that, as a commentator, you must never predict what might happen. You just lay the foundations and set the scene and let the events take place. "People can see the screen," he'd say. "You don't have to tell them he's got an eight-foot putt. They can see it for themselves." I always stuck by those principles. A good commentator should also give opinions. If his opinions aren't worth listening to, then he shouldn't be there. So if I thought it was a lousy shot and a player shirked the issue, I'd say so. Occasionally, I heard back that players thought I was too critical, but that's a commentator's job. If it's all praising, then I think it's poorly done. I also think commentators should use surnames.

SHAFTING THE SHANK

I hit shanks. Quite a few. In fact, I invented a test at the PGF factory. I was hitting a lot of shanks with my pitching wedge and I decided there had to be a reason. I reckoned that the centre of the club—its sweet spot—was not out in the middle of the blade. It was somehow near the neck ... the hozzle, or that part of the club into which the shaft is inserted.

To prove it, I had a device held by two screw points from a hanging beam and then suspended a plumb-bob. If the plumb-bob went through the centre of the iron's face, you had a good wedge, but often, with these sets that were being made, the line went through the hosel. When you swung the club, you instinctively brought the centre of the club, where the power and weight was, to the ball, and this was the hosel. We gradually solved the problem by cutting the hosel down as short as we possibly could.

Today, all irons have very short hosels. If you look at old clubs, you'll see hosels that are two or two-and-a-half inches (five to six-and-a-half centimetres) long. The reason was because it was the only way to ensure the shaft would stay in the hosel and we used to get lots of heads flying off clubs in those days. Shanking is caused, once the ball has been addressed, by bending both the knees towards the ball during the swing. Your front leg must stay straight.

I played in the South African Open one year at Royal Johannesburg and there was this fellow who came to the last hole. The clubhouse was in the middle of the course. Anyway, he shanked his second shot. Then he shanked it again. By now he was over on the ninth fairway and everybody was wondering where he'd gone. He ended up going right around the clubhouse.

GETTING A GRIP ON NICKLAUS

Jack Nicklaus was a giant because he was a winner of tournaments. He wasn't such an artistic golfer, but he was a very determined winner of championships. He burst onto the scene as the winner of the US amateur championship in 1959 and immediately challenged Arnold Palmer, who was then top dog. But an odd thing happened. Instead of being the golden boy, the American population didn't like seeing Arnold knocked off his perch, especially by a young, brash kid.

Jack was a better golfer, but Palmer remains the nation's golfing hero. This may be because their personalities were entirely different. Jack was never able to capture the hearts of the world's golfing population. Their admiration, but not their hearts. Jack had burst onto the scene using the interlocking grip. Until then, we had all used the Vardon grip, when the fingers overlap, not interlock. In the beginning, it was thought he couldn't be a champion player with such a grip, but he kept winning and eventually everyone had to admit he knew what he was doing. It sparked off a whole generation of American golfers who played with an interlocking grip and I think there was a dropping away of up-and-coming talent because of it. The reason is that it's more difficult to articulate with the interlocking grip. 95 per cent of golfers today would use the Vardon grip.

Nevertheless, Jack was immensely powerful with extremely strong legs that helped generate extra hitting power. I know him well and while we have a healthy respect for each other, we're not bosom pals. We're two vastly different people. But I'm a guest each year of his Memorial event in Ohio and that's an honour. Maybe one day it will be called the Nicklaus Classic.

HOGAN'S SLIDING FINGERS

The riddle of the sliding thumb ... well, I observed the way Ben Hogan played very closely. He was, after all, the best in the world in his time. When he played his shots, his fingers slipped around all over the place. This made me aware that the grip you start with is impossible to maintain throughout the swing. Hogan's left thumb extended, or slid, along the grip to such a point that I once observed a set of clubs he was using—around 1955 or '56—and it was quite clear that a shallow groove had worn on the grip of about an inch.

I looked at the way others played. Snead started with a long thumb and kept it for all his shots. It didn't slip, but then Snead used a glove to stop the slipping. Slipping never worried Hogan. If you see a picture taken at the end of his swing, you'll see his fingers are in quite different positions from the way they started. This gave him incredible touch and manipulation of the club head which, I think, accounted for his amazing accuracy. Hogan's retirement coincided with the development of the glove. As gloves became better made and the leather thinner, they were taken up by everybody. This stopped the movement of the thumb and people learned another way.

I understand now that you're taught to grip the club and keep that grip through the swing or to keep movement to a minimum ... to smash the ball with your arms moving and not your hands moving. I don't think that's good. So the glove played a big part in the development of the golf swing, but whether you'd call it progress I don't know, because I don't see anybody today playing as well as Ben Hogan.

A LAD FROM DOWN UNDER

When Bing Crosby does a thing, he does it properly. He foots the bill for this tournament (which is one of the biggest and most popular tournaments of the year) and the proceeds go to charity. It all started when Crosby and his friends held small get-together parties for the professionals down in San Diego before the war. It has now grown so large that newsreels, wire-photo and on-the-spot radio people gather here in force each year. Newspapers all over America want to know what Crosby is wearing and what Bob Hope said.

Hope had an auto accident last week, so he could not make it, but Crosby wore black socks throughout the tournament just to let folks know that he was sorry for him. Screen star Randolph Scott played in the tournament and partnered Dutch Harrison. Other screen stars I noticed in the gallery during the tournament were Johnny Weismuller and Esther Williams.

I met Crosby at the end of the first day. He was looking at the scoreboard and at least 200 were looking at him. I made myself known and he said he was very pleased to meet the "lad from down under". I gather that he has a liking for Australians and he has invited me to his home. All the officials wanted to apologise to me because this winter the fairways were so soggy. I said, "Thank you, but being a Melbournite I feel very much at home."

The Sun News Pictorial, January 1954

A FALLING STAR

Cary Middlecoff went from the top of the tree to the bottom in one year. He was a tall man and he got into the habit of bending both knees to get closer to the ball at impact, and it destroyed him totally. He came to Australia to play the Canada Cup with Sam Snead at Royal Melbourne in 1959. The day after, Kel Nagle and I flew up to Sydney to play an exhibition match at the Australian Golf Club. We struck a really windy day. Snead had a 69, Kel and I had about 73, Middlecoff had 82. He didn't know what to do. There's a scorecard in the clubhouse recalling it all.

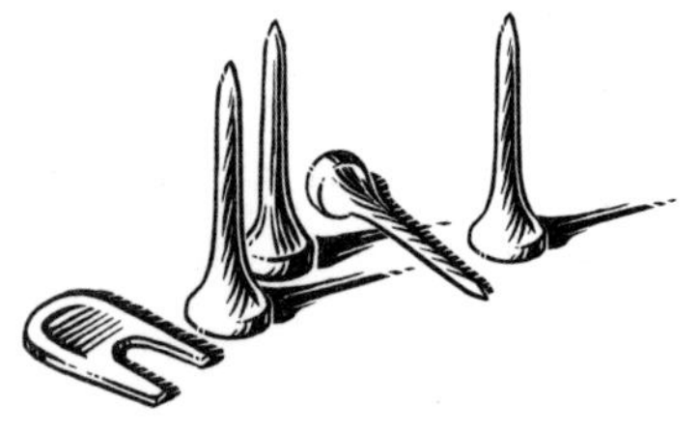

FAMILY RESEMBLANCE

Tom Watson and I were invited to the induction ceremony for the Golfing Hall of Fame in Pinehurst in 1988. It was in the form of a dinner and, before dinner, we spent a few minutes having a drink in a side room. We'd been asked to invite our families, but mine was too far away in Australia so I invited a couple of dear friends from Texas. Tom took his father. When I walked into this room, I looked at Tom's father and the hairs on my neck stood up. He looked exactly like my maternal grandfather whose name was Watson. Although my grandfather had died, these two men were not too different in age. The next time I saw Tom, I mentioned this similarity and asked him if he'd search his family roots back to Britain. The Watsons on my side came from the north-west of England—Cumberland—but he didn't seem too interested and I've never done anything about it.

THE JAMES BRAID SOCIETY

James Braid was somebody I always looked up to and admired. He won five British Opens early last century and then became a course designer, and I always liked his courses, so I developed an affinity. For the past 10 years or so, I've been president of the James Braid Society, which is a small group of people who come together to extol his virtues and keep his name where it ought to be—among the greats of the game, not only for playing but for creating courses on which the public play.

CLOSED MIND

In the public's eye, I think the US Masters has gone past the British Open in terms of importance.

I was in Austin, Texas, during a recent British Open. I walked up to a cash register to pay for something and there was a little old lady in front of me and she looked up at a television where the golf was being shown and said: "How can they ask Tiger to play on a course like that?"

HIDDEN DANGERS

In Melbourne, there's a picture of what a golf hole should look like—massive, gaping bunkers staring at you. That's not the case in Britain. They are smaller, submerged sometimes below vision height and for a very good reason—so the wind won't blow the sand away. In Melbourne, we've lost that. It's easier to open up a great expanse of sand, and although we think that's normal, it's not. It's very peculiar and it has become admired. I know that beauty is in the eye of the beholder, but this doesn't look good to me. In Melbourne, if a bunker is small and half-submerged and not quite where they want a bunker or expect to find a bunker, then it's wrong. In Britain, they're hidden away, waiting to trap you. The hidden danger is more dreaded than the obvious one.

AMERICAN RIVALS

It is just not true that I hate Americans. But as their rival in golf, I believe in keeping them at arm's length. I don't want to get any closer to men who know I am out to beat them, just as they are anxious to hammer me into the ground. Such a relationship would be an artificial and phoney one and detrimental to my mental attitude.

Golf World magazine, 1965, in an interview with Ben Wright

ROLLS AND RHYTHM

The major difference between British courses and American is that the ball bounces as far as it rolls in England. In America it doesn't. I greatly prefer close turf because I strike my shots hard downwards and I get a lower line of flight than most. Playing British-style courses requires extremely delicate judgments, rather more exacting assessments of each shot. It is not a question of fixing your eyes on the flag and swinging. It is a more sensitive game.

Sports Illustrated, July 14, 1968.

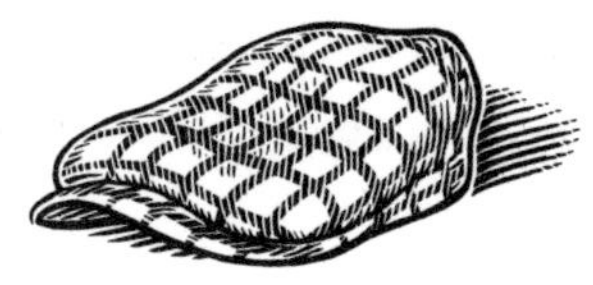

AUGUSTA MEMORIES

I was never held in awe by Augusta, the home of the US Masters. It was built on what I always thought was a very poor piece of land ... just a gentle slope ... what we in Australia would call a billy-goat track. Before it became illustrious, it wasn't universally liked by everybody who went there, but because you could only play it by invitation from Bobby Jones or those around him, it was something special. I was invited to play the Masters in 1953. At that time, it was by personal invitation. Jimmy Demaret (the Masters champion of 1940, 1947, and 1950), a good friend, suggested I should be invited. At one of the various dinners we had, Bobby Jones told me his dream for the Masters was for the field to be made up of 30 top US professionals, 30 top amateurs and 30 top foreign players. He never got his way, but this is what he had in his mind.

I always struggled with the length of Augusta. The likes of Sam Snead and Cary Middlecoff could hit a long way past me and my putting strength wasn't good enough to make up for my lack of length. But I enjoyed what I did there and I have precious memories of it. The best I did was finish fifth in 1957 six shots behind the winner Doug Ford, after starting the final day in a tie for ninth. I was doing well in 1959 (tied for seventh) when I signed for a wrong scorecard. I had the right total, but I had signed for a four-five sequence instead of the five-four and therefore I was disqualified after the third round. I played the Masters seven times from 1953 to 1961, and again in 1969, when I missed the cut.

A SICKENING GAME

I learned to play the American game over there between 1951 and 1960 and it revolted me. I have always regarded the bounce of the ball as the third dimension in golf, but the ball is not allowed to bounce in America. It is sickening to see the game reduced to something like archery or darts. Golf only becomes really difficult and challenging on hard courses. It is then that skill, not strength, counts for everything. If the ground is allowed to become firm by the natural processes of the weather, then the ball will bounce as it should, and as it was intended to do.

I turned my back on America when I saw them designing and constructing heavily watered courses over 7000 yards (6400 metres) long. Of course, I can't beat them at that kind of game, nor do I want to waste my time trying. When I saw what was happening in the States, it became my burning ambition to prove to the Americans—and to all those people who insist that to be successful, a professional must first play on their tour—that I could prepare myself to win the British Open again by playing on the British circuit. That is why I have no hesitation in calling this (the 1965 Open) by far the greatest of my successes. I have achieved a great ambition by winning with the American big three (Arnold Palmer, Jack Nicklaus and Tony Lema) in the field.

Golf World magazine, 1965, in an interview with Ben Wright

Note: In the 1965 Open Championship at Royal Birkdale, Thomson shot 285 to win by two strokes from Christy O'Connor and Brian Huggett. Lema, the defending champion was T-5 on 289, Nicklaus was T-12 on 294, and Palmer 13th. Gary Player withdrew in the final round complaining of neck soreness.

PLAYER, A GREAT PROSPECT

I saw Gary Player for the first time in January, 1956, while I was on an exhibition tour of South Africa. He was included in a match with Bobby Locke and myself at a club in Johannesburg. Locke bade me pay close attention to Player as he felt him a great prospect. Even then he was in some ways impressive, but he seemed an odd little figure with a peculiar flat swing and an unbalanced action. It was obvious at the same time that he had uncommonly intense application, something I had never seen before.

He asked me after the match whether I thought he should try his chances in Britain immediately or wait in South Africa a few more years until he thought he was ready. Both Locke and I thought that his swing was not good enough to earn him real money in the golf world, but I still saw no reason why he should wait. The experience he would gain abroad would show him whether he could make the grade or not. As history shows he did, in a most phenomenal way. He first came to Australia towards the end of that year and he won our biggest tournament ever at Yarra Yarra just before the Melbourne Olympics. By that time he was swinging a little better, although he was still very flat, and he told me that he was worried by constant pains in his back. It seemed that his long periods of practice, and his rather awkward action, were creating a strain on his back muscles and he wondered if he had many more years left at golf. I remember telling him that if he liked to stoop over a little more at the ball, he would swing rather more upright and find it a lot easier and not such a strain on his back. He practised hard to do this and by the end of the next year he had developed a very good swing indeed.

The Herald, Melbourne, 1964

OFF THE BEATEN TRACK

Kenya is the only place where animals are a serious problem. A few months ago three lions took up residence on the Karen Golf Club in Nairobi and players were advised not to play the 13th and 14th holes. Also, they have quite fierce swarms of bees there. If you hear them coming, you must throw yourself on the ground; it just won't do to stand up and flail your club at them, you know. And an odd snake or two is seen in some places.

A chap killed a cobra on the green during a pro-am tournament in Bangkok this year. Then, in Delhi, there are jackals on the course toward evening, but they are quite harmless. Delhi has had a problem with some rather ferocious monkeys, though. They don't really attack, you know, but they do menace the golfers—charging toward them with their fangs bared and chattering. The layouts range from top class to rather primitive. Any old local grass will do so long as it's green, you know. For the best of us, making a three-foot putt is no more than an even-money chance, and 34 or 35 putts around are very much an average. Their apathy toward course designing borders on ignorance because a lot of people have never seen a course anywhere else and they think theirs are quite splendid.

Sports Illustrated, July 14, 1968.

PUTTING SUCCESS

The real art of putting is being able to predict the exact path the ball should take into the hole. This is not always easy and, on certain courses, downright difficult. I believe the greens at my own course, Victoria, are as difficult to read as any greens I've come across. It is embarrassing for me not to putt well in Melbourne, my home town. For some reason or other, I always putt better elsewhere. I've always putted well in Sydney, possibly because the greens there are less sloping than in Melbourne and easier to read.

In Britain, I'm looked upon as one of the best putters ever seen there. Don't laugh, it's true. I've had some great putting success in Britain, particularly in the past few years, and always with the same stance and action. At one stage I thought of putting left-handed because it always seemed easier to me, standing over the ball, to see it as a left-hander than as a right-hander. I actually started off to play the game left-handed because they were the only sticks I could find, but luckily, I changed. Even now when putting, I find it much easier hitting left-handed. I explained this once to one of America's greatest players, John Bulla. John, like me, thought that putting left-handed was easier. He claimed it had to do with your "master" eye.

The Herald, Melbourne, 1964

A DIFFERENT SPORT

Greens should be an adventure. The game should not end when the ball is safely on the green. Up to 1953, there was one set of rules for golf. It was called "through the green" and you didn't touch the ball until it was to lift it out of the cup, unless perhaps, it was in somebody's way and you moved it to allow them to putt. But in 1953, the keepers of the game decided we needed a separate set of rules and putting became a different sport. Today, you hit a ball onto the green, mark it, pick it up, put it in your pocket, wipe it, even change it. Then, when it's your turn, you put it back. If there's an impediment, you remove it. If there's a pitch mark, you repair it. None of this happens outside the green and it shouldn't happen on the green.

IMPRESSIONABLE YOUTH

I've given up trying to pick which of the young golfers will make the grade. In his early days, I gave Gary Player no hope at all. So nowadays, I shut up and wait until they mature before I commit myself.

So much happens between the ages of 20 and 25 and I've come to the conclusion that in competitive sport you have to be lucky as a young man. It's an age when the human male seems more sensitive than a breathalyser. Victories lift an ordinary talent up where a fellow is likely to start believing in himself. At the same time, defeat seems to be so destructive. When you're older, you can take it better, see it in proper perspective, shrug it off. In general, you can say they're nicer people and then, it's easy for them to fall in with the wrong crowd. All kinds of well-meaning people will offer advice. Managers pop out of the sky like vultures. Instructors crowd around like bar flies. A young fellow can be told the most unadulterated rubbish before he's old enough to recognise it. There should be a society for the protection of young sportsmen to shield them from well-meaning idiots, who ruin a career as surely as if those concerned had taken to the bottle.

When a young golfer comes to me and says: "What do you think I should do?", I say to him: "What do you think you should do?" He will nearly always say: "Well I think I should do so and so", and I tell him: "You're right, go and do it, because the first thing you've got to learn is to make up your own mind without anybody's help." And they do. I like to see the nice, young ones get on. Trouble is, you'd really have to advise them to go around with earplugs and blinkers.

The Herald, Melbourne, 1976

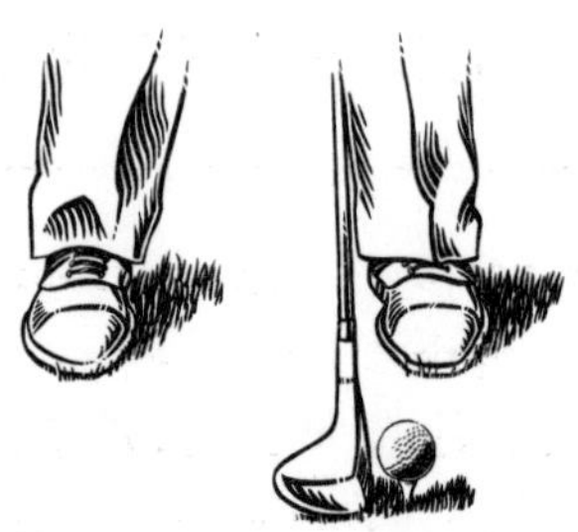

MORE THAN A GAME

A few years ago, I got a surprising request from America's leading sports magazine. Leading golfers were to give tips for a series to be called "How to gain relief from difficult shot-making problems by specific applications of the rules" and I was asked to take part. I sent a refusal and noted the series never appeared. To me, there is something unhealthy in using the rules to get out of trouble in this way—something that's certainly not in the true spirit of the game. But there's quite a different way of looking at it in the United States. There, the players are encouraged to seek rulings, probably to avoid any nasty arguments between the players themselves. Golf to them is a fiercely competitive business and much more than a game. One stroke may mean a difference of thousands of pounds won or lost. All the same, I hope the example they set is not taken up by our young golfers.

The Herald, Melbourne, 1964

FOLLOW THE RULES

All rules of golf must apply to all golfers. Since most golfers are club players, not pros, then the rules must of necessity disallow a man from keeping his own score. We mustn't forget that the important people playing golf are the club players, not the pros.

Sports Illustrated, July 14, 1968.

BIG HITTERS

Watching the young contingent of American players that Jack Nicklaus brought with him last week, one was struck by a certain similarity of style. It involved a pattern of gargantuan driving from the tee with no apparent fear or concern for the outcome, combined with an amazing propensity for recovery from what seemed to be regular departures from the straight and narrow. I venture to suggest that the frequency with which the second placegetter, Ben Crenshaw, escaped penalty after wide drives and equally wide seconds was comical. I would further suggest that had he played like that with a 1.62 inch (four centimetres) ball, he would not have finished in the first 20. I worry that if these players represent the future of the game, we are in for a decline. Excluding Hale Irwin, who seems to be in a separate small category, the main group seem to be giant hitters who are expert scramblers.

Thomson writing in *The Age* after the 1978 Australian Open, played at The Australian, Sydney

GO WITH SPEED

I don't believe the game of golf will ever disappear, but, to be critical, it is becoming too expensive and it does take too long to play.

I think the matter of cost will solve itself. Courses that are expensive to maintain will die or amalgamate with other clubs.

As for quicker golf, a 12-hole round is attractive to many people, me included as I get older.

In 1947, I went to watch the final day of the Victorian amateur championship between Eric Routley and Bobby Brown. They were to play 36 holes, starting at 9am. The morning round took just two hours and 20 minutes. Authorities wouldn't let them tee off in the afternoon until 1pm, so they had to sit around twiddling their thumbs waiting.

Speeding up play should be done voluntarily. Get on with it.

THE ART OF DESIGN

Designing a golf hole is an artistic pursuit, like painting or writing. My father was a painter ... a sketcher and a painter. He was a signwriter by profession. But in the Depression it was pretty hard to get work as a signwriter because nobody had any money to advertise. He used to do charcoal caricatures for people at the Royal Park Golf Club. There was always the smell of paint around the house. As I played more golf, I started to appreciate the architecture of a golf course. As I played these courses, I'd study them and figure out ways of playing them by minimising the risk, so when it came my turn to impose trouble I was able to do it effectively because all my life I had studied it. With age comes wisdom, and I've learned that a golf course should be pleasurable to all manner of golfers. Any course that's simply a torture test for scratch players is going to be a horror for 90 per cent of the golfing population and I think that's quite wrong. It's a natural progression from playing golf at the highest level to becoming an advisor and perhaps a designer of courses.

THE PERFECT PAR FOUR

I admire simplicity and subtlety in par fours. Believe it or not, I've always thought the first hole on the Old Course at St Andrews is the best design there is. It's so simple. There's only one feature, and that's the burn. It's close to the green and very difficult to judge the distance, especially when the wind is blowing. It has a fairway as wide as the MCG and an enormous green, but it causes tremendous havoc. I've tried to create that subtlety in things I've designed.

CLUBS SHOULD ACCEPT ADVICE

Golf clubs should have an adviser on matters pertaining to the course and its structure and the club should have confidence in that person to deliver the advice. But the vast majority of clubs become a forum of debate on what's good and what's bad for that course. It's sensible for a club to seek outside advice from someone who's competent.

IN SEARCH OF THE NEW

The whole golf world seems to be in a frenzy of course reconstruction. Here in Australia, clubs spend to surpass each other in shrugging off the sartorial tradition of the past, to replace it with a white mantle of newness. The results are, in some places, splendid, others profane.

Much of it is born of pride. We not only like to keep up, but to excel. Club committees are charged with the excitement of leaving their mark and, if taking a course by the scruff of the neck and giving it a big shake is expensive, the payback may be that those in the future will be grateful to club founders and forebears for their energies and efforts.

Not all "upgrades" are vain. Most will be born of necessity. New suburban developments are encroaching and balls are flying over fences into houses and streets. Drainage problems arise as surrounding pavements run their rainwater into fairways. Fairways and greens suffer health problems from the overgrowth of plantations of trees. And so on.

But in some cases, there is no substantial reason for reconstruction other than keeping up with the trend. Clubs that aspire to hold national championships feel obliged to increase the length of their courses in the face of the onward aerodynamics of the modern golf ball, lest their territory appear inadequate and perhaps obsolete under the onslaught of the professional players. It is a shock to most members to watch their 18 holes overwhelmed with scores in the low 60s, so it is decided something must be done.

There are now any number of advisors in the matter of

"toughening up" the course, and the advice will come down to the search for "tiger tees" further back, together with a pattern of bunkering to thwart the professionals' onslaught. Greens must be guarded so that any approach other than a high-pitched shot must be accommodated. Bunker advice will stipulate serious depth and steep faces. Size is another weapon against the buccaneers. One nationally famous course now has more than two hectares of sand within its tight boundaries. The loser in all this is the legion of high-handicapped golfers who make up the vast majority of members. And the new players with them.

Hardly anyone is about making courses more friendly, by giving relief to the less gifted in the form of more mown grass and fewer cavernous craters of sand. Or of clearing unnecessary trees within the course boundaries to let in the light and air. Where will all this end?

If there is an art to golf-course design, it is the achievement of making an 18-hole course a source of pleasure to all manner of golfers, from the best among us to the most inept. A course that is so difficult that the highest handicappers can't finish is a poor course.

ARTISTIC TEMPERAMENT

Myself, Michael Wolveridge and Ross Perrett ... we've put our touch on some 200 courses world-wide, be it one or two holes, a complete rebuild or a brand new course. The only ones I'm not proud of are the ones we didn't personally supervise. If you do the plans then hand them over to somebody else to build, inevitably it doesn't come out like you had in mind. With the others, I liken it to working with soft clay ... moulding it into the shape you want. I've always tried to impose my will on clients, which is not always possible, but I read The Fountainhead and saw the movie. Gary Cooper plays an architect and he's given a massive office building to design. The client is convinced by another jealous architect that it doesn't look right, so he makes changes. When Cooper sees what is being built without his permission, he does what I would do—he dynamites the building. I honestly believe you've got to be true to your own artistic principles. You're not an artist if you obey instructions.

MOONAH LINKS

Before Moonah, I had a chance to design a hundred or so layouts in far-flung outposts, on mostly unconducive land. Although nothing of monumental standing ever emerged, the experience was invaluable training for what was to be the Magnum Opus, the establishment of 18 holes of unique and satisfying style that would serve as a national Open Championship course.

Moonah Links was intended to be the championship course of the Australian Golf Union, in particular for the Australian Open and Australian Amateur championships. Two Open championships were played there and both were successful in that they produced worthwhile winners and they produced big crowds. Peter Lonard won in 2003 (four-round total of 279) and Robert Allenby in 2005 (four-round total of 284). It was felt the course was destined for great heights, but policy decided otherwise and Moonah hit the wall in terms of being the championship course. That's the sad truth. It's not popular with sponsors of golf and the Australian Open is in the grip of sponsors.

Is it too far away? It's as far away from Melbourne as Edinburgh is from St Andrews or Pebble Beach from San Francisco. Championship golf can survive quite successfully an hour away from a big city, but they won't try it because the risks are too great that it may fail.

A course that purports to be a classic should have a pronounced air of naturalness about it. It should not appear in any way to have been put together by moving earth. In creating such a course, holes should follow the line of least resistance whilst observing their practicality. This is easier said than done. There is ever a temptation to get fixated on one natural looking hole and ignore the integrity of the preceding and following ones. One bad hole can ruin a layout and disqualify a whole course that nearly reaches the top.

People have said that it was too tough; it was extremely tough, but it has flexibility. The essence of a championship course is that, if you don't play extremely well, you're going to get hurt. Robert Allenby shot a first round 63 and a final round 77 the year he won. Top professional golf now asks for difficult courses and low scores are not really exciting and attracting people to watch. People and players enjoy a contest between course and players.

There are any number of courses appearing on the world's stage that are two-dimensional: there is a close mown area of fairway and putting green and the rest left unkempt. This is a disappointment in that it leads the game into a shallow concept of one rigid strategy of playing that is all that a golfer needs. One has only to play on, and become familiar with, the Old Course at St Andrews to realise that a good deal of rewarding and stimulating golf is played on the ground, and the through-the-air shots are only the preparation for the real adventure.

Peter Thomson, *Moonah Links, Home of Australian Golf*

THE GROUND SPEAKS THE TRUTH

There's an old saying that "you can't make a silk purse out of a sow's ear" and it applies to golf courses.

The territory and its landform maketh the final product. Experience has shown that a course built in the mountains ends up unmistakably a mountain course, just as a layout in the wetland swamps has to be a course of lakes and ponds.

Because the list of famous classic courses is overwhelmingly dominated by British and Irish seaside links courses, it is accepted that layouts by the sea are a cut above the rest. Never mind that they are, in truth, no way superior to the best of inland courses.

DESIGNER COURSES

I can't say there has been a single influence on my philosophies about golf-course design. The character of courses is formed by the territory on which they sit. What designers do is arrange the features, and there's a certain commonality about the people who put courses together. I don't think anybody goes way off the track and survives. The best work in history has been done by Harry Colt in Britain and Donald Ross in America. I'm also a great admirer of James Braid, who designed more than 200 courses, mostly in Scotland, Yorkshire and the British Midlands. There are dozens of Braid courses still intact.

A SIMPLE RATING SYSTEM

I have begun to rate courses by the number of balls you need. For instance, if a course is a one-ball course, assuming it has all the usual features, I think it's a great course. But a 12-ball course I think is rubbish. There are plenty of those around. That's my basic criticism of Jack Nicklaus' courses. They are very much like the man himself, very serious and lacking in humor.

Golf Digest, 1994

ACCEPT FATE

I've always accepted things that happen as fate. You can't control your life. You can't map it out ahead of you. Life would be very dull if you knew what was going to happen next. I've got to this ripe old age in good health and without too many enemies. That's all one can ask.

HAPPINESS IS THE KEY

Born during the Great Depression, my life started at the bottom of the graph. The Depression formed my character as it did everyone my age. I was talking to Arnold Palmer about this just recently when he came to Sydney as part of the celebrations surrounding the Centenary of the Australian Open Championship. He and I were born one month apart and his circumstances were affected by the Depression. His family had nothing much and he has risen up to great heights of prosperity. It affects the way you look at wealth. I feel guilty spending money. I'd rather give it to my family. I owe a lot to my parents and my grandparents, whom I'm sure went without for me. I've paid them back to a small degree. I bought them the house they were renting. When my father died in 1965, I looked after my mother. She lived with us for 10 years, but she wanted to live independently, which she did until she died. I have 10 grandchildren and three or four of them are pretty talented with bat and ball. But happiness is what life's about, not whether you can hit a ball.

A FULL CIRCLE

I realised recently that, at the age of 13, I had a 25 handicap at Royal Park golf club and when I got on to my drive with my old wooden clubs, I could pound it out there about 200 metres. I have in my golf life touched the dizzy heights for a period, but now as I hide my golf from general view, I am scoring in the 80s and my best drives, metal heads and all, are reduced to about 200 metres. I have come full circle.

The Age, November 25, 2004

THE PLAYERS

By Steve Perkin

Doug Bachli (Australia)

An outstanding amateur golfer, Bachli was the first Australian to win the British Amateur title, which he did in 1954, the same year Peter Thomson won his first British Open. Both Bachli and Thomson were members of Victoria Golf Club at the time, and regular rivals during Thomson's amateur days. He died on January 6, 2000, aged 77.

Henry Cotton (England)

Born in Cheshire in 1907, Cotton is one of England's golfing legends, winning the British Open three times and representing Great Britain in four Ryder Cups. On retiring, he became an author, journalist and golf course designer. He was knighted shortly before his death on December 22, 1987 aged 80.

Jim Ferrier (Australia)

Born in 1915 and raised in Manly, Ferrier burst onto the scene in the 1930s, his amateur rivalry with Victorian Harry Williams becoming legendary. In 1938, he won both the Australian Open and the Australian Amateur Championship. If that wasn't incredible enough, he returned the next year to again win both. Ferrier became the first Australian to play the US Tour and won three events there as an amateur. He eventually turned professional and, in 1944, became an American citizen. Ferrier became the first Australian to win a Major, taking out the 1947 US PGA when, in the matchplay format, he defeated Chick Harbert 2&1 in the final. He also finished second in the 1950 US Masters behind Jimmy Demaret, before winning the 1950 and '51 Canadian Open. He was third in the 1952 Masters, and 2nd, beaten by a shot, in the 1960 USPGA. He was nicknamed "The Undertaker" because of the way he buried opponents. He died on June 13, 1986 aged 71.

Walter Hagen (U.S.)
A gifted and flamboyant character, Hagen was born in 1892. He won four British Opens, two US Opens and five US PGAs and was the first player to realise he could make money from playing successfully. He had endorsements to use certain clubs and charged considerable appearance fees for exhibition matches. Nicknamed 'Sir Walter', he died on October 6, 1969, aged 76.

Ben Hogan (U.S.)
Born in Texas in 1912, Hogan had a tough upbringing, his father committing suicide when Ben was just nine. In a career interrupted by World War II and later a near-fatal car accident, Hogan won one British Open (1953, Peter Thomson was runner-up), two US Masters, one US PGA and four US Opens. In 1965, America's sports writers voted Hogan the greatest golfer of all time. He died on July 25, 1997, aged 84.

Bobby Jones (U.S.)
The son of a lawyer, Jones was born in 1902 and was junior club champion at East Lake Golf Club in Atlanta, Georgia, at the age of nine. He won the 1923 US Open, the first of four. He also won three British Opens, one British Amateur, and five US Amateur titles. A chain smoker, he was a nervous man and often wouldn't

eat during tournaments. Jones devoted only three months in every year to golf, concentrating instead on law studies and then his law practice. He is renowned as the winner of the then Grand Slam of golf, winning the 1930 British Amateur, British Open, US Open and US Amateur. A revered figure, his legacy remains with his masterpiece Augusta National. He died on December 18, 1971, aged 69.

Bobby Locke (South Africa)
Born Arthur D'Arcy Locke in 1917, Locke was one of the greatest post World War II players. Locke is best remembered for winning four British Opens, the first in 1949, but he also won 59 tournaments in America and was third in the 1947 US Open. He also finished runner-up in Peter Thomson's first Open Championship, in 1954 at Royal Birkdale. He won the 1955 Australian Open at Brisbane's Gailes course, now not part of the Open circuit. Locke died on March 9, 1987 aged 69.

Kel Nagle (Australia)
Born in 1920, Nagle became the club professional at Pymble in Sydney's North Shore in 1951 and remained there for five years until deciding to test his talents on the world stage. He won 83 tournaments in his career, but the highlight was winning the Centenary British Open at St Andrews in 1960. Nagle teamed with Peter Thomson to win two Canada (World) Cups (1954 and 1959), he won the 1959 Australian Open at The Australian in Sydney, and seven New Zealand Opens. Nagle died on 29 January 2015, aged 94.

Byron Nelson (U.S.)
Born in Texas in 1912, Nelson turned professional in 1932 and won

the US Masters five years later. His career blossomed after World War II, when he played in 133 tournaments and finished in the top 10 in each. He had 11 consecutive tour victories in 1945 and won the US PGA in the same year. The US Tour recognises his legacy with the annual Byron Nelson Classic. He died on September 26, 2006, aged 94.

Greg Norman (Australia)
A charismatic figure on the world golfing stage, Norman won two Majors—the 1986 and 1993 British Opens—but will be remembered as someone who should have won more. He won five Australian Opens and six Australian Masters, dominating the Australian and world golf scene throughout the 1980s, during which time he was also ranked the world's number one player.

Ossie Pickworth (Australia)
Born Horace Henry Alfred Pickworth in Sydney in 1918, Ossie became one of the true characters of Australian golf. He started his career as a caddie at Manly Golf Club in Sydney but became the professional at Royal Melbourne in 1948, where he remained until 1953. He died in 1969. Pickworth won four Australian Opens and is the only player to have won three in consecutive years—1946-48. He toured overseas in 1950, failing to win the British Open, but taking out the Irish Open two weeks later. Pickworth was just 50 when he died on September 23, 1969.

Gary Player (South Africa)
Born in 1936, Player was South Africa's most successful golfer. He turned professional in 1953 and went on to win 163 tournaments world-wide, becoming one of the great golfers in the game's history.

His first professional victory was in Australia, at the 1957 Australian PGA. He won the South African Open 13 times, the Australian Open a record seven times, and won nine Majors—three British Opens, three US Masters, two US PGAs and one US Open. He is one of five players (with Jack Nicklaus, Ben Hogan, Gene Sarazen and Tiger Woods) to win a career professional Grand Slam. After joining the Seniors tour in 1985, he won nine of the senior Majors—three senior US PGA Championships, two senior US Opens, three senior British Opens, and the Senior Players' Championship. He is also the designer of more than 200 golf courses world-wide. He still tees off in many of the Majors as a guest invitee.

Dai Rees (Wales)

One of the greatest players to come from Wales, Rees was second in the 1953 (tied with Peter Thomson), 1954 (to Thomson) and 1961 British Opens. He had an outstanding Ryder Cup history, playing nine times between 1937 and 1961, captaining the team five times, with the highlight in1957 when, at Lindrick, Britain broke America's 24-year domination. He died on November 15, 1983, aged 70.

Sam Snead (U.S.)

Born in 1912, the son of a poor Virginian backwoods farmer, "Slamin'" Sam Snead won more than 80 events in America and a further 80 worldwide, but never the US Open, in which he finished second four times. In 1979, at the age of 67, he became the first player to score below his age in a PGA Tour event when he shot 67 and 66 in the Quad Cities Open. Snead died on May 23, 2002, aged 89.

Annika Sörenstam (Sweden)

Annika Sörenstam is considered one of the best golfers in the game's history. Before her retirement in 2008, aged 38, she had won 90 professional tournaments, the most wins by a female golfer. Included in that list were 72 official LPGA events, with ten of those majors.

Norman von Nida (Australia)

An outspoken character, von Nida ('The Von') , born in February, 1914, won more than 150 tournaments and set 120 course records after taking up the game at the age of nine. Like many of his era, including Eric Cremin and Ossie Pickworth, World War II interrupted his career. Nevertheless, he won four Australian PGA titles between 1946-51, and the British Masters in 1948. The same year he finished third in the British Open. He was runner-up in the same event in 1946 and 1958. He remained a lively figure in Australian golf, although failing eyesight afflicted him in his latter years. He died on May 20, 2007, aged 93.

Tiger Woods (U.S.)

Eldrick 'Tiger' Woods was the dominant force in world golf through the late 1990s and early 2000s, and remains so today. A winner of more than 50 events well before his 30th birthday, Woods was the first player to hold all four major championships at the same time—the 2000 US PGA, US Open and British Open and the 2001 Masters. His nine PGA Tour wins in 2000 were the most since Sam Snead won 11 in 1950. In 2018, Woods returned to competitive golf, aged 42, after a series of back operations.

PETER THOMSON AO CBE

Tournament Victories

1947	Australasian Foursomes Shield (with H.R. Payne)
1948	Victorian Amateur Championship
1949	Victorian Close
1950	New Zealand Open, New Zealand Masters
1951	Australian Open, New Zealand Open, Victorian Close (as a professional)
1952	Mobilco tournament (S. Africa), 1,000 Guineas (S. Africa), Victorian PGA
1953	New Zealand Open, New Zealand PGA, Victorian PGA
1954	BRITISH OPEN CHAMPIONSHIP (Royal Birkdale), World Cup (with K.D.G. Nagle), British PGA Matchplay, Ampol tournament
1955	BRITISH OPEN CHAMPIONSHIP (St Andrews), New Zealand Open, Pelaco, Speedo, Caltex, Wiseman's (S. Africa) tournaments
1956	BRITISH OPEN CHAMPIONSHIP (Hoylake, Liverpool), Dallas Centennial, Pelaco
1957	Yorkshire Evening News
1958	BRITISH OPEN CHAMPIONSHIP (Royal Lytham & St Anne's), Dunlop, Daks (UK), Pelaco
1959	World Cup (with K.D.G. Nagle), New Zealand Open, Italian Open, Spanish Open, Pelaco, Coles, Caltex (NZ)
1960	Yorkshire Evening News, New Zealand Open, German Open, Hong Kong Open, Daks and Bowmaker tournaments (UK), Wills Masters, Adelaide Advertiser
1961	British PGA Matchplay, Yorkshire Evening News, Dunlop Masters, Esso Golden (UK), New Zealand Open, NSW Open
1962	Piccadilly tournament, Martini International (UK), Yomiuri Open (Jap)
1963	Indian Open, Lakes Open
1964	Philippines Open
1965	BRITISH OPEN CHAMPIONSHIP (Royal Birkdale), New Zealand Open, Hong Kong Open, Daks tournament (UK), Caltex and Metalcraft tournaments (NZ)
1966	British PGA Matchplay, Indian Open, Caltex (NZ), Wills Masters (NZ)
1967	Australian Open, Australian PGA, British PGA Matchplay, Alcan International (UK) Hong Kong Open
1968	Dunlop Masters (UK), Victorian Open, South Australian Open
1969	Chunichi Crowns (Jap), Sax Altman tournament
1970	Martini International
1971	New Zealand Open, Dunlop tournament (Jap)
1972	Australian Open, Wills tournament, Chunichi Crowns, Pepsi tournament (Jap)
1973	Victorian Open
1976	Indian Open, Pepsi tournament (Jap)

Seniors Titles

1984	WB.TV World Seniors Invitational, PGA Seniors Championship
1985	Vintage International, American Golf Carta Blanca Johnny Mathis Classic, Mony Senior Tournament of Champions, Champions Classic, Senior Players Reunion Pro-Am, Mony Syracuse Classic, Du Maurier Champions, United Virginia Bank Seniors, Barnett Suntree Classic
1988	British PGA Seniors

Peter Thomson's British Open Record

Year	*Finish*	*Course*	*Score*	
1951	T-6th	Royal Portrush	70-75-73-75	293
1952	2nd	Royal Lytham & St Anne's	68-73-77-70	288
1953	T-2nd	Carnoustie	72-72-71-71	286
1954	**1st**	**Royal Birkdale**	**72-71-69-71**	**283**
1955	**1st**	**St Andrews**	**71-68-70-72**	**281**
1956	**1st**	**Hoylake, Liverpool**	**70-70-72-74**	**286**
1957	2nd	St Andrews	73-69-70-70	282
1958	**1st**	**Royal Lytham & St Anne's**	**66-72-67-73**	**278**
1959	T-23rd	Muirfield	74-74-72-74	294
1960	T-9th	St Andrews	72-69-75-70	286
1961	7th	Royal Birkdale	75-72-70-73	290
1962	T-6th	Royal Troon	70-77-75-70	292
1963	5th	Royal Lytham & St Anne's	67-69-71-78	285
1964	T-24th	St Andrews	79-73-72-75	299
1965	**1st**	**Royal Birkdale**	**74-68-72-71**	**285**
1966	T-8th	Muirfield	73-75-69-71	288
1967	T-8th	Hoylake, Liverpool	71-74-70-72	287
1968	T-24th	Carnoustie	77-71-78-75	301
1969	T-3rd	Royal Lytham & St Anne's	71-70-70-72	283
1970	T-9th	St Andrews	68-74-73-74	289
1971	T-9th	Royal Birkdale	70-73-73-69	285
1972	T-31st	Muirfield	71-72-74-77	294
1973	T-31st	Royal Troon	76-75-70-73	294
1974	-	Royal Lytham & St Anne's	79-81	
1975	-	Carnoustie	73-75-81	
1976	-	Royal Birkdale	75-79	
1977	T-13th	Turnberry	74-72-67-73	286
1978	T-24th	St Andrews	72-70-72-76	290
1979	T-27th	Royal Lytham & St Anne's	76-75-72-74	297
1984	-	St Andrews	72-73-76	

* From *The Complete Golfer*, by Peter Mitchell (Lothian Books, 1991)

AUTHOR BIOGRAPHIES

Peter Thomson AO CBE

Peter Thomson is widely recognised as Australia's greatest golfer. He won five British Open titles (1954, 1955, 1956, 1958 and 1965) and was the only player to win three in a row in the 20th century. He won three Australian Open crowns (1951, 1967, 1972) and was a nine-time New Zealand Open champion. He won 33 events on the Australasian circuit.

In 1988, he was elected to the World Golf Hall of Fame. He served as president of the Australian PGA from 1962 to 1994 and, in 1998, captained the International team to victory in the Presidents Cup.

He wrote regularly for *The Age* in Melbourne throughout his playing days, and during a long period as a respected commentator. At the end of his career, and then on retirement from the game, he became one of the world's leading golf course architects, working with John Harris, Mike Wolveridge, Ross Perrett, and in his later years, with Tim Lobb. Peter retired from active participation in the firm in 2016.

From 1979-1984, he was the founding chairman of Odyssey House, an institution providing support for those seeking to break a habit of addiction. Peter died on June 20, 2018, aged 88.

Steve Perkin

Steve Perkin is a writer, author and passionate social golfer. He has covered many major sporting events in Australia and overseas.

He has had stints as sports editor of *The Sunday Age*, executive producer of *The Footy Show,* wrote the *In Black & White* column for the *Herald Sun* for many years and has edited a group of business and retail magazines.

He is currently freelancing and lecturing in sports journalism.